THE TREADMILL OF PRODUCTION

Advancing the Sociological Imagination
A Series from Paradigm Publishers

Edited by Bernard Phillips and J. David Knottnerus

Goffman Unbound! A New Paradigm for Social Science
By Thomas J. Scheff (2006)

The Invisible Crisis of Contemporary Society: Reconstructing Sociology's Fundamental Assumptions
By Bernard Phillips and Louis C. Johnston (2007)

Understanding Terrorism: Building on the Sociological Imagination
Edited by Bernard Phillips (2007)

Armageddon or Evolution? The Scientific Method and Escalating World Problems
By Bernard Phillips (2008)

Postmodern Cowboy: C. Wright Mills and a New 21st-Century Sociology
By Keith Kerr (2008)

Struggles before Brown: *Early Civil Rights Protests and Their Significance Today*
By Jean Van Delinder (2008)

The Treadmill of Production: Injustice and Unsustainability in the Global Economy
By Kenneth A. Gould, David N. Pellow, and Allan Schnaiberg (2008)

Bureaucratic Culture and Escalating World Problems: Advancing the Sociological Imagination
Edited by J. David Knottnerus and Bernard Phillips (2009)

Forthcoming

Ritual as a Missing Link within Sociology: Structural Ritualization Theory and Research
By J. David Knottnerus (2009)

THE TREADMILL OF PRODUCTION

INJUSTICE AND UNSUSTAINABILITY IN THE GLOBAL ECONOMY

Kenneth A. Gould, David N. Pellow,
Allan Schnaiberg

Routledge
Taylor & Francis Group

LONDON AND NEW YORK

First published 2008 by Paradigm Publishers

Published 2016 by Routledge
2 Park Square, Milton Park, Abingdon, Oxon OX14 4RN
711 Third Avenue, New York, NY 10017, USA

Routledge is an imprint of the Taylor & Francis Group, an informa business

Copyright © 2008 , Taylor & Francis.

Notice:
Product or corporate names may be trademarks or registered trademarks, and are used only for identification and explanation without intent to infringe.

Library of Congress Cataloging-in-Publication Data

Gould, Kenneth Alan.
 The treadmill of production : injustice and unsustainability in the global economy / Kenneth A. Gould, David N. Pellow, Allan Schnaiberg.
    p. cm. — (Advancing the sociological imagination)
 Includes bibliographical references and index.
 ISBN 978-1-59451-506-4 (hardcover : alk. paper)
 ISBN 978-1-59451-507-1 (paperback : alk. paper)
 1. Environmentalism. 2. Environmental policy. 3. Environmental degradation.
4. Social ecology. I. Pellow, David N., 1969– II. Schnaiberg, Allan. III. Title.
 GE197.G685 2008
 333.72—dc22

                                                                    2007044446

Designed and typeset by Straight Creek Bookmakers.

ISBN 13: 978-1-59451-507-1 (pbk)
ISBN 13: 978-1-59451-506-4 (hbk)

For Frederick H. Buttel, 1948-2005,
whose mastery of political-economic dynamics
continues to inspire us.

Contents

Preface

THE RELATIONSHIP BETWEEN THE GLOBAL ECOSYSTEM and increasingly global social systems is more problematic today than at any point in history. In this book we present a theoretical framework, the treadmill of production, which seeks to explain why socioenvironmental dynamics are increasingly out of balance, and why national and global *social institutions* have failed to adequately respond to the rapid disorganization of natural material life support systems. Paradoxically, we note that over the years in which the theory has been revised and refined, much U.S. scholarship and the focus of a growing share of U.S. environmental movements have increasingly shifted toward addressing environmental issues as a *personal problem* (Mills 1959). For example, much has been written about how to recycle our *household* waste (Weinberg et al. 2000). In similar manner, many community groups have tried to negotiate local agreements with toxic waste producers in their own "back yard" (Weinberg 1997). Even former "President-elect" Al Gore's Live Earth concerts, intended to raise awareness about global climate change, emphasized the "little things" people can do as *individuals* to reduce *their* impacts on the environment, with little note made of the possibility of collective action to address this social problem. With the attention of two billion global citizens, the Live Earth event failed to offer a framework for understanding the systemic nature of the climate crisis or any other aspect of the social system–ecosystem interaction, and that is precisely what the treadmill of production theory aims to do.

While the treadmill of production theory was initially proposed in 1980, we see that it continues to explain many of the unresolved environmental and social problems in the contemporary world. Its original analysis of *U.S.* environmental problems boldly argued that one major factor helped shift how our environment changed from a situation representing a *surplus* to U.S. society to one in which we became more aware of the *scarcity* of many of our environmental amenities. This factor was the growing level of profits increasingly invested in new technologies rather than in expanding employment or raising the status of workers. The hallmark of the emergent U.S. production system was an accelerating rate of displacement of production workers. These workers were replaced by new technologies that were being systematically developed by large-scale organizations for the first time in history.

Such new technologies were being developed both by university researchers and by industrial research and development teams in firms themselves. In addition, government support of basic and applied research in the post-1945 period changed the previous "little science" into "big science" (Price 1986). A large share of this research was designed by and for the use of the military, with treadmill firms producing much of it. Ironically, it was a former general (and president), Dwight D. Eisenhower, who cautioned Americans in 1961 about the growing *military-industrial complex* emerging in the United States:

> This conjunction of an immense military establishment and a large arms industry is new in the American experience. The total influence—economic, political, even spiritual—is felt in every city, every State house, every office of the Federal government. We recognize the imperative need for this development. Yet we must not fail to comprehend its grave implications. Our toil, resources and livelihood are all involved; so is the very structure of our society.
>
> In the councils of government, we must guard against the acquisition of unwarranted influence, whether sought or unsought, by the military-industrial complex. The potential for the disastrous rise of misplaced power exists and will persist.
>
> We must never let the weight of this combination endanger our liberties or democratic processes. We should take nothing for granted. Only an alert and knowledgeable citizenry can compel

the proper meshing of the huge industrial and military machinery of defense with our peaceful methods and goals, so that security and liberty may prosper together.

In some ways, Eisenhower's statement paid the first political attention to the emergent treadmill of production. As Schnaiberg (1977) argued, there was a huge expansion of *production science,* which involved narrower social objectives that were increasingly being tested in industrial pilot plants. This science was mobilized to accelerate the treadmill firms' accumulation of profits.

In contrast, very little funding was allocated to *impact science*: research on the social distribution of economic goods and bads was not being considered, nor were the rising levels of ecological bads. Interestingly, when Rachel Carson (1962) published her popular warning book, *Silent Spring,* much of the information about environmental disruption had in fact been noted earlier by her scientific colleagues in government and industry. They feared retribution if they came forward publicly with such news of ecological disruptions caused by production processes and some military applications. It was not until the rise of somewhat politicized environmental movements in the mid- to late 1960s that a new constituency was created for scientists who were documenting the negative environmental impacts of the treadmill. By the 1970s, the U.S. federal government created the Council on Environmental Quality, the Environmental Protection Agency, and the National Environmental Policy Act. While some viewed these as *institutionalized environmental movement organizations* (Morrison 1986), subsequent history has demonstrated that these and other "environmental" entities are in continuous tension and conflict with the dominant treadmill of production.

Initially, treadmill theory explained how the U.S. production system had changed in ways that substantially increased environmental disruptions during the *1945-1980* period. Its theory of increasing capital-intensification of production was also focused on how the new technologies substituted higher levels of *energy* and a wider array of *chemicals* for human labor. In the post–World War II period, producers and their investors viewed the natural environment as a system with a *surplus* of natural resources, increasingly available to producers. Because of the treadmill system's acceleration during this period, though, environmental systems began to display new *scarcities*: the air was unhealthy to breathe, the water was increasingly unsuitable to drink, and large portions of plant and animal habitats were disappearing under the higher levels of treadmill production.

While new social movements arose to pressure producers and government agencies to limit the use of ecosystems for production feedstocks and waste disposal sinks, these movements faced growing resistance from producers and their investors. Extracting environmental resources for eventual marketplace activities was quite profitable—even though new environmental disruptions occurred for human and plant/animal species. As Schnaiberg (1980: 5) noted, it was not a situation in which "we" were "saving the environment." Rather, the treadmill theory was about the distribution of *risks* from environmental disruption, and the distribution of *power* involved in perpetuating or changing this disruption. We sought to provide the "development of alternative paradigmatic assumptions which promise to help resolve basic contradictions between present ideals and practices within the academic world and beyond" (Phillips and Johnston 2007). In this context, the treadmill of production was a *political-economic* theory of conflicting *social* interests and *environmental* outcomes.

The treadmill theory of 1980 U.S. realities represented a framework that we have subsequently extended into later periods and across a wider array of societies. This book explores both the initial conflicts analyzed for the 1945–1980 period, as well as the policy conflicts for the 1964–1980 period. More importantly, perhaps, this book stresses the extension of the treadmill from a U.S.-based theory to one that has become more relevant for the growing levels of transnational production associated with *globalization*. Yet resistance to acknowledging the reality of the treadmill's predictions emerged from the very outset of the initial model, with the emergence of more conservative, protreadmill regimes in the northern societies. This had the effect of limiting political discourse about the model by activists, and increasing the reluctance of scholars to directly confront the political-economic nature of U.S. and other societies' environmental problems. "The extraordinary language of social science—invoking perception in the momentary situation, and sensitivity to physical, personality and social structures—would necessarily be involved ... in order for the individual to penetrate the complexity of any given momentary scene." (Phillips 2008)

With the extension of treadmill theory to the globalization of trade and production, there was a mixture of resistance from dominant political regimes and agencies, coupled with some new audiences among southern environmental and social activist groups. For while political-economic analysis remains unpopular (if not deviant) within the American academy, there is far more openness to the treadmill's implications by analysts and activists more accustomed to structural reforms.

Schnaiberg's collaboration with a group of Northwestern University-trained scholars led to some modifications of his earlier premises in a series of books (1994, 1996, 2000) and articles (1991-2007). Many of our later articles, which outlined how to make the treadmill of production theory more useful, were published in a series of journals and books. A number of these are not easily accessible by students and our colleagues (especially in the era of reduced library budgets).

To acquaint students and other social scientists with the framework of the treadmill, we have written this book, which reports on and synthesizes the evolution of a contemporary treadmill theory of production. In addition to this short book, there are Web sites that make available (through PDF files) a number of the original articles (e.g., http://www.northwestern.edu/ipr/people/schnaibergpapers.html; http://www.sociology.northwestern.edu/faculty/schnaiberg/Schnaibergpapandpub.htm).

The original work on this book was prepared for the Symposium on Environment and the Treadmill of Production, University of Wisconsin, Madison, October 31–November 1, 2003. The host and moderator of the symposium was the late Frederick H. Buttel, to whom we dedicate this monograph. Numerous suggestions for revising the initial paper came from a number of participants, including, especially, John Bellamy Foster, who helped craft a special edition of *Organization and Environment* around the symposium papers.

This book addresses a number of questions that have been raised over the years about the origins, structure, and application of the treadmill of production theory. Because the theory has been evolving to incorporate new empirical findings and alternative conceptual premises, this work should be viewed as a starting, rather than an ending, point for using the treadmill of production theory in analyses of socioenvironmental problems and solutions. We encourage readers who still have unanswered questions to contact any of us, and we will try to address them as best we can.

Acknowledgments

WE DEDICATE THIS WORK to Frederick Buttel for a number of reasons. Most immediately, we acknowledge his untimely death in January 2005 as a loss to us and to the field of critical sociology. Among his other contributions to our work, he organized a conference at the University of Wisconsin in October 2003, focused on the treadmill of production theory. This book grew out of our presentation at that conference. But we also draw on Professor Buttel's critical introduction, in which he argued that the evolving theory of the treadmill had not been readily available to a wider audience. Furthermore, we have followed the arguments of his critique in developing this manuscript. Finally, the intellectual craftsmanship of Fred's large corpus of work has contributed to our understanding of the treadmill's utility (and some of its limitations).

Beyond this, our work here draws upon the contributions of Adam Weinberg to the evolution and application of the treadmill theory in his own work and in our collaborations with him. In the wider scholarly community, we are indebted to numerous students and younger social scientists who have offered us professional support and enthusiastic endorsement of the value of the treadmill theory for their own constructions of social reality and for their own analytic work. This has sustained our efforts in the face of political pressures that have often marginalized the treadmill in social and environmental analyses.

Each of us has also learned from one another in the years that we have been collaborating. As Schnaiberg has noted often, "it is a source of great pleasure that I am able to turn to my former students as colleagues who can now tutor me."

Finally, those closest to us have been supportive during periods of considerable frustration and uncertainty. But they have also shared in the joys of creating a growing body of work and a socially valuable vision of the world we all inhabit.

PART I

Origins of the Treadmill Theory

An early illustration of the Treadmill of Production by Greg Curry, 1981.
(Courtesy of Greg Curry)

CHAPTER 1

The Treadmill of Production as an Outcome of Scientific Methods

The Development of the Treadmill Theory

DURING THE LATE 1970s, much of the commentary about the causes of environmental problems was provided by natural scientists. There were a small number of social scientists beginning to work in this area, most of whom had originally worked in other sociological subspecialties: demography, agricultural development, or sociology of science, among others. The writings of this aggregation of commentators provided a wide array of competing arguments about the origins of environmental degradation. Among them were rising population levels, "runaway" technology, consumer greed, and/or new "research and development" by corporate and government scientists and technologists.

Schnaiberg (1980) attempted to incorporate this array of arguments into a single work. Rather than just proposing some other single "cause" of environmental decay, he used the existing literature to begin a search for a grounded theory (Glaser and Strauss 1967) of ecological destruction in modern industrial society. This theory essentially involved an application of a scientific method

3

to a complex set of changes in the society-environment relationship. A key component involved the incorporation of each of the existing arguments and an attempt to discern whether historical and contemporary facts were consistent with a causal statement about the origins of an environmental problem.

As with many persistent social issues that C. Wright Mills (1959) explored, the complex history of environmental degradation afforded many puzzles that no single theory could explain. Some pollution problems of mining, for example, had been noted in the sixteenth century (Mumford 1963). Yet there was little doubt that both the intensity and extensity of ecosystem disruptions had greatly accelerated during the middle of the twentieth century (Melosi 2001). From the timing and nature of this shift, Schnaiberg (1980: 5) constructed a theory that he felt was both plausible (i.e., consistent with historical observations) and compelling (i.e., one that seemed to track historical changes with a better fit than any of the existing arguments).

Myopia exists when social scientists concentrate only on the environmental movement, not on the social context from which it arises. Abstractions about our anti-ecological culture are not much help in addressing the problem. Schnaiberg's approach was to seek an explanation of the social roots of expanded production through an analysis of social institutions involved in the creation and allocation of social surplus. What social forces induce ever-higher levels of industrialization and extraction of resources? (Schnaiberg 1980: 4)

The Development of Environmental Social Movements

During the 1960s and 1970s, the United States experienced the rise of the modern environmental movement. While it emerged in a period in which many new mass social movements appeared, the early history of these social organizations showed that they did not overlap much with the environmental movement. Bell's (1962) controversial argument that traditional political alignments were disappearing by the 1950s was somewhat validated by the emergence of new antipoverty, antiwar, antiracist, and profeminist movements. Yet a careful analysis of the membership of national environmental movement organizations in the late 1970s showed little overlap by "environmentalists" with any of these other societal concerns (Mitchell 1980).

One of the factors that led Schnaiberg to construct analytically a new theory of environmental change was actually the extraordinary diversity of "environmental movements." His early work (1973) outlined at least four categories of such movements: cosmetologists, meliorists, reformers, and radicals. While other social movements also entailed an array of activists, Schnaiberg's analysis outlined important differences. Yet applying this insight to his newly constructed theory, he was somewhat chagrined to realize that the treadmill of production theory was likely to find only a limited audience (which the later analyses in this book confirm). Indeed, he already stated (1980: 5) that the problem was not that people wanted to "save the environment": "the question must always be asked: *for whom*, and *from whom* has it been protected?" [italics ours]

Studying Consciousness Raising and Lowering about the Environmental Impacts of the Treadmill

In a recent work, Szasz (2007) has raised a provocative question about why many Americans have chosen to make private provisions for their health and welfare. In doing so, they have avoided offering strong support for government regulation of the treadmill's impact on the environment, including its impacts on human health. In Mills's (1959) framework, they have chosen to treat only those private troubles generated by the treadmill and largely have ignored most of the greater social issues that make such troubles so common. One example Szasz offers is the private use of bottled water, rather than the emergence of collective political demand for safe water systems in communities. He offers arguments about why this private path has been followed and the public path largely ignored. Other examples abound, including the purchasing of "Green" consumer products without seeking deeper changes in production processes and industrial organizations.

Schnaiberg (1980: 4) had earlier puzzled openly about that:

> How does our social organization obscure the realities of result-
> ing environmental degradation? In what ways do productive and
> governmental organizations treat environmental critics and their
> claims? How does this explain discrepancies between public
> complacency regarding environmental problems and the growing
> concerns of many policy analysts?

It should be noted that since this statement in 1980, current assessments of the environmental movement have indicated that
its potency exists far more in the European Union than in the
United States. Nowhere is this clearer than on the issue of global
warming, where the U.S. government (and even some environmental organizations) has chosen to treat the issue as scientifically "unproven," as well as insolvable (Begley 2007). And most
of those organizations and elected officials who have embraced
the cause of challenging global warming are unwilling to argue
for the transformative (i.e., massive) changes required to achieve
such a goal. Clearly, within the European context, the increasing disjuncture between the functioning of social systems and
ecosystems has been imagined far more sociologically than it
has within the context of the United States. This should not be
surprising since the United States is ideologically more prone to
locating both the causes of troubles and the remedies for troubles
at the level of the individual (i.e., contrasociologically).

This concern about the consciousness of citizens and movement groups and their capacity to frame environmental issues
sociologically drove us to focus on many of these problems, both
in this work and in earlier ones. The treadmill is not just grounded
in causal space; its reception by social leaders directly contributes
to whether it is amenable to social change.

Individual Responses to the Treadmill, and Its Institutional Grounding: Consciousness Construction and Destruction

In an earlier analysis, Schnaiberg (1993) outlined the modal
positions of individuals and groups opposing the treadmill's

antienvironmental outcomes. While doing so, he laid out a synthesis of much of the existing literature outlining both what environmental movements faced in attempting to act as well as what environmentally conscious individuals were exposed to. The items in Table 1, drawn from a diversity of literature, are organized to make the resistance by treadmill proponents clearer to the reader. While there is no guarantee that this represents a scientific sample of such conflicts, it resonated with the experiences we have all had in supporting and working with environmental movement organizations (Gould 1991, 1992, 1993, 1994; Pellow 1999; Tsoukalas and Gould 1997).

From this perspective, it becomes clearer that "saving the environment" in the face of structurally imbedded opposing institutional interests is a much more problematic and challenging action for citizens to take (St. Clair 2007).

Components of the Theory

Schnaiberg introduced the treadmill of production theory to address why U.S. environmental degradation had increased so rapidly after World War II. He argued that a growing level of capital available for investments and its changing investment allocation together produced a substantial increase in demand for natural resources. Essentially, the major change outlined in the theory was that more capital was accumulating in Western economies and it was being applied to replacing production labor with new technologies to increase profits. These new technologies required far more energy and/or chemicals to replace earlier, more labor-intensive processes, thus producing deeper levels of ecological disorganization than ever before. New technologies emerged from the organization of scientific and technological research in universities and research institutes as well as from the new "research and development" departments of large firms. Moreover, unlike the prior use of labor, the new technologies represented forms of sunk capital. To further increase profits, managers needed to increase and sustain production levels (because worker inputs could be cut back more readily, as opposed to the fixed costs of machine operations).

8

Table 1. Competing Claims about the Environmental Problems of the Treadmill

Environmentalist claim	Producer counterclaim
Problem severity issues	
1. Ecological disorganization is being produced	No ecological disorganization being produced
2. Major ecological disruption is "known": we do not need to postpone action for future research	Some ecological disruption already is occurring, but it is minor; we need costly ecological and community research to establish any "problem"
Causal issues	
3. The disorganization is socially produced, not "naturally occurring"	There is some disorganization, but it is not really socially produced
4. Mechanisms exist to reduce or eliminate this disorganization without stopping or slowing societal growth	The ecological disorganization is socially produced, but it is an inevitable by-product of societal growth
Benefit-cost issues	
5. Technologically feasible ways exist to control the disorganization already available or near at hand	We are currently unable to control this disorganization and need costly production and ecological research before any production options can be weighed
6. We can easily afford to implement the corrective technologies through implementation of regulatory rules, including fines for producers who violate them	Some corrective options are possible, but they are costly to use, and producers need some incentives to make them feasible
7. Social benefits from environmental protection are far greater than the relatively modest costs of implementing them	The costs of correcting these ecological problems really exceed any benefits of melioration
*Cost-benefit issues**	
8. Social and ecological benefits of recycling [reuse] are greater than economic costs	Economic and ecological benefits of recycling [remanufacturing] are greater than economic costs
9. Social and ecological benefits of energy conservation [reduced use] outweigh economic costs	Economic and ecological benefits of energy conservation [increased efficiency] outweigh economic costs

*Issue arena of relatively low conflict

How Did the Treadmill Theory Differ from Other Contemporary Theories of Environmental Degradation?

When Schnaiberg first developed the treadmill of production theory in 1976, this was an exercise in empirical induction (Glaser and Strauss 1967). At that time, natural scientists or engineers conducted most of the public discussions of environmental degradation. They addressed both the causes of environmental decay and the solutions. While both entailed social-structural issues, none of the observers had any social science insights. Neither their radical nor their conservative analyses reflected any social science data, theories, or concepts. As a social scientist with a technical/scientific background, Schnaiberg tried to understand why U.S. environmental conditions had declined so precipitously since World War II. He accepted the bioecological "facts" of the late 1960s and early 1970s: there was indeed an ecological problem, and it would ultimately have some social consequences (the rationale for his commitment to this work).

No matter where Schnaiberg turned or what he read, the dominant narrative always seemed to start with changes in economic production as the major determinant of the trajectory of ecosystem impacts. From a logical perspective, production changes were the efficient causes of environmental disruption. So his initial question was transformed into: why had the quantities and/or qualities of U.S. production changed so drastically from 1945-1975?

Some analysts claimed that it was the growth in population that required a production increase. As a sometime demographer, it was clear to Schnaiberg that, while there had been a baby boom during this period, the rise in energy and material use vastly outstripped population growth. Demographic explanations, he argued, were often appealing mainly because we had detailed records of population characteristics. Thus, we could trace the rise in population along with the rise in some forms of pollution (see Ehrlich 1971). Ignoring the methodological dictum that we need to distinguish causation from mere correlation, it became easy for many early analysts to take an environmental statistic, divide it by the level of population, and come up with a "per capita environmental impact" assessment. This *ratio* was treated as if it were an analytic *rate* of how much each individual actually added to environmental degradation. In fact, this rate was nothing other than a form of circular argument or tautological reasoning. Certainly, it was true that a growing population did require some additional production and natural resources, but this was only a small component of the changes in environmental degradation from 1945–1980.

Others argued that the qualitative changes in production had been the result of "runaway technology." But from the outset, as a former engineer, Schnaiberg knew that technology did not "run away"; rather, deliberation, time, and (especially) investment are required to change technology. A number of those arguing about these technological changes were themselves natural scientists (and even engineers). They sought to trace environmental degradation to its origins in the production system—as a kind of "efficient" cause. But they had a naive perspective on how and why these technological changes occurred. They never linked these changes to both the novel investment by corporations in research and development departments and the growth in government and industry grants to university science and engineering research (Price 1986). They saw only the surface of change—a rapidly changing set of technologies, which appeared to lack deliberate social control.

Hence they appeared on the surface to be runaway, rather than planned, changes (Meadows et al. 1972). Of these two arguments, it was technological change theory that Schnaiberg began to trace. What he soon realized was that there had indeed been substantial technological change in the third quarter of the twentieth century, which required huge amounts of capital. Where did this capital come from? He began to realize that this capital component arose from a combination of factors including a substantial postwar economic boom, which led to increased production and profits. These profits were disproportionately applied to new physical technologies.

In effect, the treadmill theory synthesized changes both in the *forces* of production and the *relations* of production (using Karl Marx's concepts). It further integrated these changes with the creation of ecosystem disruptions due to the changing scale and form of societal production. It was inductively uncovered, not guided by any particular theory of political economy.

The Economy as the Driver of Environmental Degradation

The treadmill of production was thus primarily an economic change theory, but it was one that had direct implications for natural resource extraction as well as for the opportunity structure for workers. In essence, the treadmill component recognized that the nature of capital investment led to greater demand for natural resources, for a given level of social welfare (including wages and social expenditures). Each round of investment weakened the employment situation for production workers and worsened environmental conditions, but it increased profits. For production workers, this treadmill implied that increasing investment was needed to employ each one. For ecosystems, each level of resource extraction became commodified into new profits and new investments, which led to still more rapid increases in demand for ecosystem elements.

Treadmill theory focused on the social, economic, and environmental conditions for *stakeholders* (workers and community residents). Simultaneously, expansion of the treadmill structure enhanced the economic and political power of *shareholders* (investors and managers). Political gains for shareholders included a growing capacity to induce both government and labor unions to support still more investment of this sort, to employ displaced and new workers, and to augment state tax revenues. Over time, this increased political power of shareholders was enhanced by their capacity to obtain still more political support for treadmill expansion, through an expanded use of profits for direct (and indirect) campaign contributions. The initial treadmill theory was published in 1980, at the onset of a new era of political conservatism in the United States. The new antienvironmental and antisocial policies of the Reagan administration dominating the political landscape offered a hostile social environment for the adoption of the treadmill theory among both scholars and activists (see below). Since 1980, in fact, most of those using the treadmill theory in their research on socioenvironmental dynamics have been younger scholars, especially younger scholars in the "global south" (see below) whose political consciousness has been shaped by witnessing the social and environmental impacts of the neoliberal era that Reagan ushered in.

The treadmill theory presented an image of a society running in place, not moving forward. It represented a decrease in the social efficiency of the productive system. This decreased social efficiency of natural resource use produced a shift toward vastly increased rates of ecosystem depletion (resource extraction) and ecosystem pollution (dumping of wastes into ecosystems). Moreover, workers and their families politically supported the expansion of this new capital-intensive form of production. As the growing treadmill cast off workers, their major consciousness was that accelerating this new form of investment was necessary and sufficient for "social progress." Economic growth was viewed as the primary solution to the negative social impacts of economic growth. Thus, each round of socially dislocating growth generated increased, rather than decreased, social support for allocating investment to accelerating the treadmill of production.

Politicians were induced to provide direct and indirect support for such expansion: they received strong support for doing this from investor-managerial groups. And they received public support from workers and their unions, who supported virtually any and all kinds of "economic development." While some workers and their unions attempted to resist these processes, even they were under growing economic, social, and political pressure to accept this as the *only* path to social progress, although reluctantly. Any resistance to this change was labeled as antediluvian, Luddite, old-fashioned, reactionary, and doomed to failure (see below) by a variety of economic and political representatives. Ironically, this rapid growth in support occurred despite considerable doubt about the future of the U.S. peacetime economy after the end of World War II (with fear of a return to the economic depression of the 1930s). Within five years, though, the accumulated savings from the wartime period were mobilized to create vast new infrastructural and manufacturing investments to stimulate production expansion. Through the period of 1945–1960, the promises of unlimited energy (especially atomic energy) and newly accessible mineral and other extractive resources (especially petroleum) led to social and political inattention to ecological limits and unthinking support for unlimited economic expansion. Early twentieth-century attention to "sustained yield" utilitarian approaches to land and water (Hays 1968) were largely dismissed, and emerging pollution problems were not well researched or managed. Waste was mostly moved into the commons, with spillage into water systems, dispersal into the air, and dumping into land systems at some distance from cities. These presaged the perspective of "limits to growth," which emerged in the late 1960s and 1970s. They were largely ignored, in favor of attending to economic expansion.

Social Class, Economic History, and the Emergence of a Treadmill Economy

Part of this lack of attention was facilitated by the growing segregation of the social classes. Middleclass workers, who benefited from the expansion of the treadmill, largely moved to emerging bedroom suburbs. Blue-collar workers and many craftspeople lived in cities or small company towns, where they struggled with rising local pollution and community health problems, juxtaposed with their need to preserve their jobs. While pollution was a negative externality for both white-collar and blue-collar workers, it was geographically and socially removed from many members of the rising educated middle class, yet increasingly dispersed into communities of the working class. The middle class lived upwind and upstream from polluting enterprises. Blue-collar workers were induced and/or coerced to live downwind and downstream or adjacent to polluted communities because of their lower property costs and the limited wages of the workers. This class-based distribution of residential location insulated production decision makers from the health and environmental consequences of their decisions (Gould 2006).

Ironically, one of the precursors of the treadmill model was an early argument of Barry Commoner, a socially progressive biologist (and later a Green Party presidential candidate), who helped expand ecological consciousness in the United States. His ecological analysis of declining capital productivity (1977) paralleled our own work. This was in stark contrast to the standard economic and managerial focus on worker productivity. When Commoner wrote in the 1970s and even in the current political-economic climate, the obsession with increasing worker productivity has dominated many policies. From the standpoint of the treadmill theory, increasing worker productivity is often associated with accelerating the treadmill—producing yet fewer worker benefits at a given rate of natural resource extraction. Indeed, raising worker productivity was the central dynamic of corporate decision making in the initial theorizing about the treadmill of production. The treadmill process aimed to displace many workers—through an increase in physical capital per worker (and hence potential environmental impact per worker), using profits to raise production technology. The goal was to enhance profitability or return on investment. Inherent in this process was a substantial increase in energy needs and in chemical waste discharge, as well as elimination of habitats for flora and fauna. Since 1945, habitat destruction has probably been the best marker of treadmill expansion (through resource extraction or waste disposal).

There were two outcomes of this process that affected workers. For most people, these changes eventually led to a decline in wages and job opportunities, what Harrison (1994) has termed the "low road to development." Part of this scenario was accomplished by crushing worker unionization through job blackmail (Kazis and Grossman 1982). Another major factor was rooted in the practice of closing U.S. plants and moving them to locations in the global south, where labor was substantially cheaper, workers were nonunionized, and workers and politicians were desperate for new employment possibilities for their expanding young populations. From maquiladoras in Mexico, to sweatshops and factories elsewhere, the rate of return on investment rose substantially. U.S. workers waited desperately for new investment, as previously noted, while workers abroad accepted new employment, which appeared to raise their living standards somewhat. Both situations increase the potential for intensified environmental damage, often by elimination of existing environmental protection regimes, at the same time as they produce greater economic volatility.

Yet there was a smaller class of workers who experienced this process as a "high road to development" (Harrison 1994). *Their* wages, skills, and careers were enhanced by their incorporation into the new physical (and electronic) technological systems. This included workers directly involved both in the new production and also in marketing, financial analysis, and customer service. In recent years, though, this high road has become increasingly susceptible to the core logic of the treadmill. For middle-level managers and educated professionals of all types, there are strong pressures to increase "worker productivity" to sustain corporate profitability by reducing expenses.

Paradoxes of the Treadmill

Beyond the core logic of the treadmill, this model generally encourages analysts to take into account a range of factors that produce environmental insults as well as to understand how these factors make environmental policy making so complex. The treadmill model underscores the importance of paying attention to dialectics and contradictions in the behaviors of individuals, groups, the state, and industry. When we develop a sociological understanding of the constraints and choices within which individuals and institutions exist, environmental conflicts and solutions become clearer yet more inaccessible. For example, although the majority of U.S. workers would like to live and work in safer, cleaner environments, they are often either unable or unwilling to take direct action to achieve these realities. Although most Americans indicate that quality time away from work is an important goal in their lives, they tend to spend more time working every year. Likewise, elected officials must maintain their legitimacy with the voting public and secure the "monopoly" powers of the state (Tilly 1978); yet they routinely make decisions that erode state power and public legitimacy. Ratifying free trade agreements, which undermine the ability of nation-states (and subsidiary forms of government) to exercise social control, starkly illustrates this contradiction. Industry needs to secure and maintain the obedience of its workers, but managers engage in practices that violate the social contract and worker trust.

The treadmill model also underscores the importance of social inequality, power, and conflict as key parts of the impacts of social systems on the environment. Many scholars simply surveyed people's environmental attitudes and concerns. But the treadmill theory offered not just an analysis of what people thought about the environment but also a focus on the behaviors of social institutions and their impacts upon the natural world.[1]

Using the treadmill model as our tool, we have often taken positions that are unpopular or that run counter to the prevailing consensus on a number of topics. For example, there is a scholarly tendency to celebrate (and overstate) the influence of the environmental, antitoxics, and environmental justice movements (Dunlap and Mertig 1992; Szasz 1994; Bullard 1993). In contrast, we have used the treadmill model squarely to face the reality that these social forces were (and remain) at a major power disadvantage vis-à-vis political and economic elites. Indeed, we believe that environmental sustainability/protection around the globe has declined substantially, despite the work of these movements.

This sort of "bad-news" reporting in scholarly circles is generally unappealing and often frustrating for those of us who would like to believe that both the environment and our societies are moving toward a state of sustainability. The same dynamic applies to the debate between treadmill theorists and proponents of ecological modernization, with the latter adopting a fundamentally upbeat outlook on industrial practices (Garcia Johnson 2000), despite continued and intensified ecological destruction around the globe. This approach has, at times, met with both acceptance and resistance from activists as well, who have a social investment in reports that the global ecological crisis is serious, but who also seek affirmation that their actions are having a positive impact on ecosystems.

Treadmill theory encourages scholars, activists, and others to explore deeply, rather than to gloss over, the contradictions in social responses to environmental disorganization. These paradoxical institutional and individual responses illustrate most clearly the dynamics of social system–ecosystem relations. Ultimately, it is in the resolution of such paradoxes that ecologically sustainable and socially just solutions may be found.

A "Do Not Litter" sign planted in the midst of a mountain top removal during a coal mining operation in Eastern Kentucky, 1996. The entire top of the mountain was removed to access a coal seam. (photo by Ken Gould)

CHAPTER 2

Why Does the Theory Focus on Production Rather Than on Consumption?

TREADMILL THEORY AT ITS CORE was a political-economic theory: it focused first on the distribution of power (Lukes 1974) to influence societal production. From there, Schnaiberg added the focus on the distribution of opportunities and costs presented in this new production system, for workers, managers, and investors. The focus then expanded to trace how this distribution of power and impotence affected both the *ecological* systems in which communities were embedded and the *economic, social,* and *biological* conditions of workers.

Schnaiberg (1980) initially outlined the substantial change in technologies in the third quarter of the twentieth century. The newer technologies were inevitably more energy- and chemical-intensive on the one hand and less labor-intensive on the other. Capital mobilization for these technologies arose from a substantial postwar economic boom, which led to increased production and profits. These profits were used disproportionately to develop and introduce new physical technologies. To amortize their fixed as well as their operating costs, however, production in general

19

had to be substantially increased, which, in turn, increased the demand for natural resources, both energy and other. Once in place, the expanded production of the new technologies substantially raised both the volume of and the toxicity of wastes (due to greater use of chemicals).

From the outset, then, the treadmill of *production* focused on decision making in the realm of *production*. Its model of socioenvironmental dynamics emphasized production rather than consumption. While individual consumers may be the ultimate purchasers of *some* of the products of the new technologies, decisions about the allocation of technologies is the realm of production managers and owners. Decisions about types of technologies, the use of labor, and volumes of production are made outside the realm of consumers. Individuals, communities, states, and corporations consume only the outputs of a given production technology. The majority of what social systems consume must be extracted from nature (extraction being the leading edge of any production process), and then further processed to generate a final product. While consumers can accept or reject these products, they have no influence over the allocation of capital to productive technologies. Thus, it is within the production process where the initial interaction of social systems with ecosystems occurs and where the key decisions about the nature of social system–ecosystem relationships are made.

Many popular economic theories postulate the responsiveness of supply to demand. Yet it is in the decision to *provide* supply, and the means by which that supply is provided, where social systems and ecosystems first collide. Production decisions may or may not be influenced by anticipated consumption demand. But the relationship between production and ecosystems, which provides the total stock of potential materials for production, is a direct one. In contrast, the relationship between consumption and ecosystems is indirect. Consumption decisions are made in the context of previous production decisions as well as prior social distribution decisions.

By recognizing the relationships between economic structure and political power, the treadmill model contextualizes the role of consumer decisions within the material parameters of their political economy. Consumer choice devolves from (1) the constraints of specific prior production decisions, (2) specific prior economic distribution decisions, and (3) a specific distribution of policy- and decision-making power. To place consumption decisions first in our analyses would obscure the power relations embedded in the political economy. Henry Ford's famous "consumer choice" comes to mind: he told the public they could purchase any color Model T car they wanted, "as long as it's black!" "Consumer behavior" studies have few theories about the power underlying them. Obscuring the distribution of power serves the discipline of neoclassical economics quite well in its reinforcement of the status quo. Such obfuscation violates the critical analytical and empirical requirements of sociology, however.

The mechanisms through which human needs and desires are formed are largely determined by preexisting conditions of production, beyond the basic biophysical needs of humans as living organisms (food, warmth, shelter, social interaction). Desires are socially constructed, and material desires are largely constructed by material producers through various forms of cultural production (Schiller 1996). The transformation of socially constructed material desires into human needs is a result of social processes, which are heavily influenced by those who control production decisions. Contrary to classical and neoclassical economic theories that posit that consumer preferences determine the contour of markets, consumer behavior is consciously being shaped by industry. The "gospel of mass consumption" was the successful construction of consumer desires not by consumers themselves but by the captains of industry and their collaborators in the advertising sector. Thus, the extraordinary rise in productive output after World War II was complemented by a rise in personal consumption among U.S. citizens.

Consumers may opt not to buy specific items. But they are not empowered by market processes to determine how such items will and will not be produced. In this sense, they are not seriously empowered to alter the ecological impacts of production decisions. Even the degree to which individual, community, state, and corporate consumers are free to choose whether to purchase available products is itself contested. A key dimension of the exercise of power is the ability to influence, if not dictate, the choices of those less powerful (Lukes 1974). Individual choices not to consume products generated by powerful actors involve an underlying power struggle between highly unequal contenders.

It may be argued that individual, community, state, and corporate consumers may alter or terminate specific forms of production by consumer boycotts. However, these collective victories still do not empower consumers to determine the *means* by which alternatives will be produced, or even what alternatives will be produced. Indeed, it is possible that no alternative will be produced, thus freeing consumer capital to be funneled into other items already made available by producers. In theory, the decision not to consume may terminate the production of specific products. In rarer cases, such a decision may even terminate specific forms of production. Yet few if any examples of either of these cases have occurred directly through consumer choice, and only a handful have been implemented through political pressure from social movement organizations (politically organized interest groups of consumers). Although the famous grape boycott succeeded in raising social consciousness about working conditions among farm laborers, it was not an economic success.

Again, however, the decision of which *alternative* forms of production will be offered consumers is not in their hands. It remains in the hands of a small minority of powerful individuals (treadmill elites) who are empowered by their access to production capital. It is in those decisions where social systems (the producers' access to capital and labor, and their assessment of potential liability, profitability, and marketability)[1] and ecosystems (the producers' access to natural resource inputs and ecosystem waste sinks) first interact.

The consumption decisions of individuals, communities, states, and corporations are secondary to production decisions, which generate the material and cultural contexts in which consumption decisions are made. Therefore, any socioenvironmental theory that focuses primarily on consumption decisions necessarily overlooks the primary social system–ecosystem interactions, the primary social actors determining the nature of those interactions, and the exercise of political and economic power manifest in making those determinations. In short, analyses of socioenvironmental dynamics that begin with consumption tend to miss the importance of social structure and the distribution of power stemming from the political economy.

Such producer decisions are influenced by the regulations imposed by the state, and by negotiations with their labor forces. This is why the treadmill of production model emphasizes the role of nonelite individuals as *citizens* (polity) and *workers* (labor) rather than as consumers (Gould et al. 1996). It is also why the model emphasizes collective actions (such as those by nongovernmental organizations [NGOs] or social movements) over individual choices/actions. Nonelite treadmill participants alter the nature of social system–ecosystem interactions by pressuring private capital and/or state decision makers to choose more proenvironmental production processes. Much of the limited success in achieving treadmill alteration in the post–World War II era was achieved through pressure by social movement groups. For example, most, if not all, environmental legislation passed during this time was the result of progressive forces seeking to slow the excesses of treadmill institutions. Treadmill nonelites may use their role in physical production to directly induce capital actors to alter their production processes. Organized labor has done so sometimes for environmental concerns—or, more frequently, because of occupational safety and health concerns associated with ecologically disruptive technologies (Schnaiberg 1986).

Thus, the treadmill model implies that more democratic ownership and control over production would ameliorate social and ecological problems more than attempts to control rates of consumption or choice of certain products. Consumers can choose Pepsi or Coke or some low-calorie, alternative soft drink. Yet this is largely irrelevant if the ownership and control over all these products is in the hands of producers who are simultaneously displacing workers, taxing the state's resources, and placing great burdens on the ecosystem. Clothing is another "consumption" example. Unless consumers in the global north make their own clothes, they leave producers the appealing option of having virtually all clothing made in sweatshops that exploit laborers and typically produce various ecological disruptions (in both agriculture and transportation). As long as owners are free to invest in low-wage countries (or employ low-wage immigrants in industrial countries), consumers exercise little control over these production processes.

Only when activists have collectively organized citizens in consuming countries (and workers in producing countries) will there be a possibility of more political "choice" with regard to sweatshop labor. Consumers have become relevant actors only when these movements have organized them into boycotts, which then serve largely as consciousness-raising functions.

Recycle, Reuse, Reduce?

Unfortunately, consumerist approaches to the problem of the treadmill almost never consider the goal of deceleration. The question of how much we are consuming (i.e., growth) is rarely challenged. The focus is on changing only what goods we are consuming. This is perhaps not surprising, as consumerist approaches are fundamentally about protecting the right to consume as much as they are about corporate and social responsibility. For example, the major campaigns many national environmental groups spearheaded in the 1980s and 1990s emphasized recycling (an environmentally problematic industrial process) (Weinberg et al. 2000). Yet they largely eschewed emphasis on the more socially and ecologically effective practices of materials reuse and reduction. In earlier analyses, we demonstrated that as long as companies harvest timber at increasing rates (i.e., increases in production) it matters little whether environmentally conscious residents (i.e., consumers) are recycling their waste because any potential gains from residential recycling are offset by increases in production. This type of analysis preceded and informed research on "commodity chains," by noting the multiple points at which social, political, and economic forces affect each other and environmental protection efforts.

Some recycling campaigns have, however, focused on production. For example, in 2003, a national coalition of environmental organizations (including the now defunct Grass Roots Recycling Network) successfully pressured a number of computer manufacturers to begin recycling their computers at the end of their lifecycle (i.e., when consumers would normally throw them away).

This appeared to be a major victory—in that recycling computers is probably better than dumping thousands of them in landfills. But the proposal failed to challenge the imperative of industrial growth at computer firms and actually reinforced it. Although the recycling proposal was more progressive than most others because it required producers to build recycling/reuse options into their design of new computers, its major limitation was the failure to address the growth in both consumption and manufacturing and the decreased life expectancy of the product.

The treadmill model argues that the collective bases of historical success in altering aspects of the political economy arises only through direct or indirect political conflict with state and capital elites. The role of treadmill nonelites as individual consumers is at the tail end of the system, not at the leading end. In contrast, their collective roles as citizens and workers offer the potential to alter the production decisions of elites, who essentially control social system–ecosystem interactions. The treadmill model at least suggests the need for a more radical restructuring of the political economy. Citizen-workers need to achieve more control over production decisions. In this perspective, prolonged engagement in enduring conflicts with powerful treadmill decision makers may be effective (Schnaiberg and Gould 2000).

Production is the locus at which we can observe and measure the degree of ecological withdrawals and additions as well as potential solutions. Yet production is also where industry leaders will fight the most to maintain their autonomy from the state, environmentalists, and labor. Control over production is the critical battleground for industrialists generally, and it is where the waste industry, in particular, drew the line in the struggle over the Resource Conservation and Recovery Act (RCRA) of 1976. Industry successfully fought to shift federal mandates for recycling outside the production process onto consumers and states in an effort to protect profitability and control over production. Globally, industry leaders engage in a range of actions to ensure this control, from relocation to avoid unionization to the use of private and state armies to intimidate, torture, and execute opponents (Gedicks 2001).

For them, production is legitimately the exclusive province only of the owner/management/shareholder class, with virtually no input from other affected parties. For example, one day in 1992, Latino workers at Versatronex, a Silicon Valley computer firm, won the right to engage in collective bargaining with the company (by order of the National Labor Relations Board [NLRB]). The firm immediately announced that it was declaring bankruptcy and closing down the next month. Silicon Valley business leaders made it clear that their firms would remain union free or they would simply move elsewhere.

The treadmill is organized under the premise that producers, not consumers, are the major driving factor in the political economy. Consumers, for example, would prefer to be able to purchase environmentally responsible products, but this decision is ultimately up to producers. However, we should never ignore the impact of consumer behavior.[2] Growth in urban pollution has been rising, in part, because of increased vehicle ownership and mileage. These have offset a large portion of the emission reductions gained from motor vehicle controls. This is a classic illustration of the treadmill of production at work. In view of the unforeseen growth in automobile use, combined with the serious air pollution problems in many urban areas, Congress has made significant changes to the motor vehicle provisions of the 1977 Clean Air Act, but the core problem of growth in production and consumption of automobiles is left unchallenged.[3]

A policy focus on consumption is almost always the easy path: it generally absolves industry and the state of responsibility for a host of problems. A consumption focus:

- leaves production largely undisturbed;
- fails to challenge the fundamental structure of the industry in question;
- often blames poor populations for not engaging in "enlightened," "responsible," and "conscious" consumer practices; and
- leaves the analysis of power unexplored or inverted.

Although the treadmill model's emphasis remains on production, it could also be said that it addresses the way that producers and other stakeholders literally *consume* the ecosystem and *become* consumed by the (il)logic and seductions of the treadmill.

As such, it could be said that we have redefined or broadened our notions of what "consumption" is (industrial and collective versus personal/individual). The study of the social, economic, and environmental impacts of personal consumption is gaining greater visibility (see Clapp 2001; Park 2003; Schor and Holt 2000), and we welcome this development. However, scholars emphasizing this phase of the product lifecycle would do well to remember that it is just that—a *cycle*, which begins with production.

Contaminated creek outside the Y-12 National Security Complex, a nuclear weapons production facility in Oak Ridge, Tennessee, 1992. The primary contaminant of concern in the creek is mercury. (photo by Ken Gould)

CHAPTER 3

Is the Treadmill a Dialectical or a Linear Change Theory?

SOME CRITICS OF TREADMILL THEORY argue that it appears to be a theory of linear change. There is some irony in this because most of the "standard" economic theories (especially neoliberalism and free trade) are almost exclusively linear in their presentations. Indeed, they are treated as axioms (to be believed in), not theories (to be tested). Much of contemporary economic theory is, in fact, a kind of morality tale (Krugman 2002). The arguments supporting it are rarely subjected to empirical scrutiny.

There are two quite distinct aspects of our research concerning the treadmill. First, we note that the initial *theory* of the treadmill was a historical model of changes that seemed to have appeared in the United States and other industrial societies. Alongside this historical pattern, Schnaiberg initially proposed that there were many political-economic alternatives to the social and ecological impacts of an accelerating treadmill. As workers confronted new social and economic restrictions, they would act politically to favor policies offsetting the treadmill tendencies. Likewise, as environmental degradation began to have more pronounced effects on communities and families, citizen-workers would act to reduce relatively unrestricted economic control over ecosystems. In both cases, Schnaiberg predicted that social and political actions would serve to reduce the growing influence of treadmill institutions and ideologies. Among other strategies, he listed the following possibilities (1980: 228–229):

- replacement of large corporate employment with small-scale entrepreneurialism;
- direct state provision of essential public services (e.g., transportation, education);
- decrease in profit seeking in favor of other goals of corporate entities;
- reduction of capital available for technological innovation because of rising labor costs;
- government subsidies for provision of employment by the private sector;
- expansion of state agencies to absorb displaced workers;
- an increase in inventories and reduction in capital accumulation and investment because of unsold goods;
- direction of profits into salaries or bonuses, for example, instead of into additional investments;
- support for an increase in demand by the public sector to offset decreased consumer demand in the private sector;
- wider acceptance of high unemployment levels; and
- increased taxation to reduce capital investment and enhance social services.

As part of his initial work, Schnaiberg described the *dialectical* dimensions of economic growth and environmental impacts. He outlined three syntheses—economic, managed (planned) scarcity, and ecological. Each of these would influence treadmill forces in a different way within the political-economic system. The treadmill was quintessentially an economic synthesis. By 1975–1980, though, there were significant environmental protection policies in place, which Schnaiberg labeled as planned scarcity, because the state would limit the degree to which treadmill institutions had access to ecosystems. At the other extreme, the ecological synthesis entailed the state's substantial control over ecosystems, without regard for the issues of profitability and wages/

employment. Treadmill institutions *theoretically* would have to restructure their activities to provide employment and wages and to protect crucial aspects of ecosystem functioning. It was unclear then (and now) how this would occur, given the recent history of treadmill expansion and the growing cultural commitment to this process as the major social option for treadmill elites. Interestingly, the ecological synthesis bears surprising similarity to sustainable development, the successor to the intermediate technology development trajectory that Schumacher (1973) detailed decades ago. Equally important, though, is that in the last 28 years, there appears to be very limited movement toward sustainable development. Even the proposals of the Kyoto conference, which quite modestly proposed limiting production of greenhouse gases to reduce global warming, failed to find support in the United States (and a complex mixture of support and opposition elsewhere).

So the theory of the treadmill entailed an inherently dialectical system, in which social forces benefiting from its expansion would engage in political contests with those diminished by such expansion. In a recent paper, we have termed this the "societal-environmental dialectic" because society seeks both economic growth and environmental protection, and yet these goals exist in tension with one another (Schnaiberg 2004). And in the last 28 years, there have indeed been local, national, and multinational contests challenging the treadmill. Yet it is our assessment that the *empirical history* of the 1976–2008 period is one in which the treadmill has only occasionally been slowed. It is more accurate to suggest that its *rate of growth* has sometimes been slowed, and only by political opposition or market downturns. One of Schnaiberg's (1980) naive expectations was that the publication of the treadmill model would lead to substantial mobilization of *opposition* to the treadmill.

Yet history has belied his expectations. Despite the plethora of state regulations, the empowering force of global environmental treaties and conventions, and the emergent networks of social movements (nongovernmental organizations), it is hard to argue empirically that the treadmill has shrunk. There *have* been a few modest victories, such as the increased energy efficiency of many productive enterprises and the reduction of air, water, and land pollution in a variety of locales, especially in the United

States and some other industrial societies. There *have* been more courses in business schools devoted to "environmental management" and new social theories about ecological modernization as a form of reflexive modernity (Beck 1992; Mol 1995). And yes, there has been an enormous increase in postconsumer recycling in industrial societies (Weinberg et al. 2000).

Yet treadmill structures have adapted quite well to these new challenges. We could state boldly that *increasing the return on investment has displaced every other social and environmental goal* in this period. Moreover, this principle has become dominant in more societies through the forms of globalization controlled by investors from the previously industrial societies. Indeed, this principle is increasingly dominating all forms of globalization, despite the resistance by socially and environmentally progressive forces in northern and western Europe as well as by indigenous peoples everywhere (Collinson 1996; Goldman 1998). We could go even further: it seems apparent that *more of human activities throughout the world fall under the influence of the treadmill institutions and logic* than was true in 1980. In one sense, this growing monoculture of the production system is expressly antithetical to the goal of sustainable development or to the even more modest goal of a managed scarcity model (Stretton 1976). From the perspective of the treadmill, the media representation of economic change is profoundly misleading. When "productivity" increases, especially through increased use of technology per worker, this is actually an acceleration of the treadmill—leading to higher production levels and greater profits, but with fewer workers. In effect, this increases the demands for more treadmill investment by greater numbers of displaced workers. As we initially drafted this book, more reporters noted that job woes persisted even as the U.S. economy recovered, in what became known infamously as the "jobless recovery" (Krugman 2003: 73–75). This concept raises troubling questions about what exactly a "recovery" is if it excludes employment security for workers. Paradoxically, consumer debt is at an all-time high; this is a scenario that we have documented and envisioned earlier (Schnaiberg and Gould 2000: ch. 6).

So we can argue that the treadmill theory was dialectical but that the empirical history of the United States and global political economies since 1980 have been only weakly so. Indeed, rather than the treadmill's expanding linearly over this period, it has expanded exponentially. As we note later, this calls for a serious reevaluation of various proposals for environmental protection, including the recent arguments of ecological modernization theorists (Mol 1995).

The treadmill's expansion is evident in at least two forms: (1) the increasing level of social inequality in the U.S. class structure, within U.S. firms, and between the global north and south today; and (2) the growth in natural resource extraction and polluting activities around the globe. We consider the rise in social inequality first.

The Haves, the Have-Mores, and the Have-Nots

Among the major industrialized nations, the United States holds the dubious distinction of being the one country with the greatest gap between rich and poor, and the divide has been growing steadily over time. The gap between rich and poor has only widened since Lyndon B. Johnson launched his War on Poverty in the 1960s. According to a report by the independent Congressional Budget Office, the wealthiest 1 percent of U.S. families received an average annual income of $1,016,900 in 1997. The bottom 20 percent of income earners brought in an average of just $11,400 that year (Hays 2003: 121). The top 10 percent of income earners had a median net worth of $833,600 while the bottom 20 percent had just $7,900 (Crenshaw 2003). Any way you cut it, the portrait of social inequality in the United States is stark. In 1998, the wealthiest 0.1 percent of families (about 1,300 households) reported the same income as the poorest 20 million households—earning 300 times the income of average families (Wallach and Woodall 2004: 152). If working people are faring so poorly, how are their bosses doing? The ratio of earnings between the top 100 U.S. chief executive officers and the average worker jumped from 39 to 1 in 1970 to 1,000 to 1 in 1998 (Krugman 2002). And this predates the negatively redistributive Bush-Cheney administration tax cuts.

These income statistics are stunning but are even outdone when one considers the effect of *wealth*—property, investments, assets, etc.—on inequality. In the year 2000, the top 1 percent of U.S. households owned 40 percent of the nation's wealth. These class differences are also compounded by racial and gender inequalities that are passed down across generations (Oliver and Shapiro 1995; Amott and Matthaei 1991).

The continued rise in inequality in the United States, while exceptionally strong, is mirrored by global trends:

> The richest one tenth of the world's population earned a median income 77 times that of the world's poorest one-tenth in 1980. By 1999, however, the richest one-tenth earned 122 times that of the poorest one-tenth. Entire regions of the developing world are falling alarmingly behind the wealthiest countries that compose the Organization for Economic Cooperation and Development (OECD). Sub-Saharan Africa's per capita income was one-sixth that of OECD countries in 1975 but fell to one-fourteenth of OECD per capita income in 2000. Over the same period, per capita income in Latin America and the Caribbean fell from less than one-half that of OECD countries to less than one-third, and Arab countries' per capita income fell from one-quarter that of OECD countries to one-fifth. (Wallach and Woodall 2004: 9–10)

The income gap between the one-fifth of those in the richest countries and the one-fifth in the poorest was 74 to 1 in 1997, up from 60 to 1 in 1990 and 30 to 1 in 1960. Again, this is evidence that inequalities are not only extant but growing over time. By 1997, the richest 20 percent of the world's population captured 86 percent of the world's income, with the poorest 20 percent holding onto a mere 1 percent (United Nations Development Program 1999: 3). The richest 1 percent of the world's population earned more income than the poorest 60 percent (GroundWork 2002). Because inequality (economic, political, and social) is a driving force of both environmental decay and social conflict, a constant increase in global socioeconomic inequality cannot be socially or ecologically sustainable.

The major dynamics of the treadmill of production are perhaps best demonstrated in free-trade accords, which are lauded as boons for democracy and economic progress by U.S. and European heads of state. The reality reveals quite the opposite trend, however. As in the United States, studies have found conclusively that, around the world, trade liberalization agreements are linked to increasing social inequality, decline in real wages, and rising unemployment.

> In almost all developing countries that have undertaken rapid trade liberalization, wage inequality has increased, most often in the context of declining industrial employment of unskilled workers and large absolute falls in their real wages, on the order of 20–30 percent in Latin American countries. (United Nations Conference on Trade and Development 1998)

Free trade agreements primarily benefit wealthier nations and investors, international financial institutions, and transnational corporations (TNCs) (Gould, Schnaiberg, and Weinberg 1995). The economic and political power of transnational corporations is formidable indeed. As Tony Clarke writes, "Forty-seven of the top one hundred economies of the world are actually transnational corporations; 70 percent of global trade is controlled by just five hundred corporations; and a mere 1 percent of the TNCs on this planet own half the stock of foreign direct investment" (Clarke 1996). As some scholars have noted, this kind of economic power easily translates into political power as well, where foreign investors essentially constitute a "virtual senate" that can veto many nations' efforts to enact progressive labor, environmental, or economic legislation (Pellow 2001).

The treadmill marches on, and social inequality is only one component of the problem. The associated rising level of toxics production, pollution, and natural resource extraction is staggering.

Natural Resource Extraction and Increasing Pollution and Toxicity

Many scholars and politicians would like to think that we live in a high-tech computer age, marked by postmodern politics where social structures and material wealth matter less than in previous eras (for a good critique, see Boggs 2003; Philo and Miller 2001). Nothing could be further from the truth. We, particularly in the global north, are as dependent on natural resources as we have ever been. In fact, that dependence is deepening as we increase our reliance on ecosystems—particularly those outside our bio-regions—to fuel the global economy. For example, between 1992 and 1998, U.S. imports of finished steel jumped from 13 million to 35 million net tons (Wayne 2001); between 1985 and 1996, Latin American nations extracted and exported 2.7 billion tons of basic resources, most of them nonrenewable (Pellow and Park 2002). The United Kingdom reflects a similar pattern:

> In the UK, iron consumption has increased twenty-fold since 1900; the global production of aluminum has risen from 1.5 million tonnes in 1950 to 20 million tonnes today [1999]. In the decade 1984-1995 ... aluminum consumption in the UK rose from 497,000 tonnes to 636,000; steel consumption increased from 14,330,000 to 15,090,000 and wood and paper consumption more than doubled, from 41 million to 93 million tonnes. (Huws 1999)

The thirst for oil from nations and regions around the planet (e.g., western and southern Africa, North America, Latin America, Central and East Asia, and the Middle East) continues to fuel wars, unsustainable consumer and industrial practices, ecological devastation, and poverty (Gedicks 2001). Likewise, the thirst for clean water and water for industrial production purposes has led to epic political battles in California, Texas, Mexico, Israel, Bolivia, India, and elsewhere. We are consuming and polluting the most basic building block of life at an unsustainable rate (Shiva 2002; Barlow and Clarke 2002). Steel, oil, gold, coal, water, timber, and other natural resources are being consumed to a degree never before witnessed in human history. All these withdrawals are also associated with additions—pollution—and have serious consequences for human health.

Toxic materials exposure from industrial production and consumer goods has caused genetic defects, reproductive disorders, cancers, neurological damage, and the destruction of the immune system in human populations around the world. This is not an aberration: modern industries are highly toxic. "Wherever there is industry, there are hazardous wastes" (Goldman 1991: 196-197).

The evidence of risk and disease associated with industrialization abounds. The U.S. Centers for Disease Control and Prevention (CDC) released a study in January 2003 in which they tested more than 9,000 individuals across the United States and found pesticides in 100 percent of their bodies (CDC 2003). Polybrominated diphenyl ethers (PBDEs) are a little known class of neurotoxic chemicals embedded in computers, televisions, cars, furniture, and other common products used by consumers in the global north every day. PBDEs are ubiquitous not only because they are contained in so many consumer products but also because they leak into the environment during production, use, and disposal. As a result, they are found in house dust, indoor and outdoor air, watersheds, and the body tissues of dozens of animal species around the world, including humans. In the United States, Europe, and Canada, women's breast milk has been found to have high levels of PBDEs, and most U.S. residents are believed to carry unsafe levels of this chemical in their bodies (Lunder and Sharp, http://www.ewg.org/reports/taintedcatch/es.php).

Despite the relatively more powerful environmental and labor movement communities in Europe, nations there continue to pollute with an alarming intensity. One in five persons employed in EU nations is exposed to carcinogenic agents on the job. Cancer, asthma, and neuropsychiatric disorders are some of the illnesses associated with the 100,000 chemicals and biological agents marketed in the European Union, according to the European Agency for Safety and Health at Work. Approximately two-thirds of the 30,000 most commonly used chemicals in the EU have not been fully tested for their potential health impacts on humans or the environment. New chemicals introduced since 1981 undergo such tests, but older chemicals remain untested (ENS 2003). The question of intergenerational impacts is raised here because our generation, more than any previous one, has greater potential to harm future generations (irreparably).

The treadmill of production has thus expanded enormously over the last sixty years, with increasing levels of social inequality within and between nations; exacerbating class, race, and gender divisions in societies; and a greater degree of natural resource extraction and pollution than ever before with dire consequences for the health of both humans and the ecosystem. This is the result of a globalized treadmill.

PART II

Evolution and Application of the Theory

A billboard advertisement for Pepsi Cola featuring the image of Jesus from the Christ the Redeemer statue atop Corcovado, an iconic Rio landmark. Rio de Janeiro, Brazil, 2000. (photo by Ken Gould)

CHAPTER 4

How Has the Treadmill Theory Changed under Growing Globalization of Production since 1980?

THERE HAS BEEN LITTLE APPLICATION of the treadmill logic to systematic analyses of globalization, other than our own recent work. Even in Schnaiberg's initial work (1980), however, he was already concentrating on *political-economic* changes taking place within the global economy. In many ways, even his earliest primitive analysis presaged the effects of the North American Free Trade Agreement (NAFTA) and the changes in the World Trade Organization (WTO): a rise in investment in less-developed countries would eventually lead to a reduction in consumer spending and, hence, to a reduction of U.S.-based production for the U.S. market. In turn, these dynamics should have reduced the environmental impact of U.S. production and afforded more potential for ecosystems to recover from past disruption (if the state had intervened to pressure the treadmill institutions to do this).

To trace the role of the treadmill under conditions of globalization, however, requires some careful distinctions. One of our recent puzzles was that the rising imbalance of trade payments has left the United States as the world's largest debtor nation! Yet there has been little political attention to this situation, which could, according to macroeconomic theories of trade, lead to a total collapse of the U.S. treadmill structure. Why has this aberration caused so little political ripple?

A partial answer seems to require us to distinguish between states and global interest groups. When the "United States" experiences a vast array of imports for a much lower array of exports, what does this actually mean? To *whom* is "the United States in debt?" Ultimately, the answer seems to be, in part, to U.S.-based investors and managers, who have shifted production abroad and imported the results of this "foreign production" (foreign investors have taken on an increasing level of debt in U.S. investments in recent years as well). Because the treadmill's major goal is increasing return on investment after all, U.S. investors and managers desire to reduce U.S. investment in favor of greater investment abroad precisely because of the attraction of lower overseas wages (and often lower environmental protections, as shown in the NAFTA debates).

In addition to directly benefiting U.S. investors and managers, this system has the effect of pacifying U.S. environmentalists (through reductions in local production and pollution). In this era of downsizing and wage reductions, the importation of more cheaply produced "foreign" goods has permitted less affluent U.S. workers to buffer themselves somewhat against their wage losses or wage stagnation. Interestingly, a third benefit is strengthening the claims of U.S.-based investors and managers that they need labor and environmental concessions from workers and the state to remain "competitive" (often with their own overseas production organizations!).

All of this should caution analysts (including ourselves) to be exceedingly careful in conceptualizing the treadmill influences within "globalization." Indeed, even the term *globalization* is misleading because it implies interstate relationships as constituents of the new economic order. Yet it is much more accurate to examine the competing interests involved in the process and to understand how each has succeeded or failed to offset some of the social and environmental pressures of treadmill organizations and culture. Such interests include U.S. workers, environmentalists, and political representatives; and foreign workers, environmentalists, and political representatives, among others. We will not trace all the connections but will note a simple environmental impact principle that underlies globalization.

In general, capital seems to have shifted more toward environmental degradation through production abroad than it has to environmental protection within the United States or in countries with U.S. investment. Moreover, there appears to be a shadow "pricing" of environmental disruption by globalizing treadmill interests. They are willing only grudgingly to reduce or ameliorate pollution from their production facilities. But in return they absolutely refuse to accept any limits to production (actually, profit limits). Thus, we in the United States have cleaner streams and rivers and some reduction in air pollution. But in return, habitat destruction due to logging, mining, and agriculture has increased dramatically since 1980, both in the United States and in U.S.-investor locales overseas (at least as measured by ecological indicators of habitat destruction and species extinction). The export of hazardous chemical wastes and the transfer of toxic technologies have followed the same pattern, producing extreme occupational health problems and ecological disruptions in the global south as the U.S. Environmental Protection Agency (EPA) celebrates improvements in certain environmental indicators as if they were primarily the result of developing cleaner production domestically (Clapp 2001; Daykin and Doyal 1999).

Indeed, in an age where there have been increasing calls for sustainable development and sustainable biodiversity, the loss of habitat and associated species in countries of the global south has accelerated rapidly since the United Nations Conference on Environment and Development (the Earth Summit) in Rio de Janeiro in 1992. While some of this may be due to population growth (Rudel 1993), the majority of habitat loss appears to have come by way of increased investment in extractive industries (agricultural, mining, and especially forestry) (Rudel 1993; Sonnenfeld 2000). This is the major cause of habitat destruction, despite recent and visible declarations and policy mobilization by organizations whose main mission is environmental sustainability through population reduction and control (e.g., see the Population

Institute, Federation for American Immigration Reform, Sierra Club). Loss of species diversity is further accelerated by the pollution associated with the greater processing and manufacturing activity (e.g., refineries and petroleum distribution). Many of the rates of natural resource extraction (e.g., oil mining) and pollution (e.g., power plant emissions) have declined in the United States and other industrial societies. But the globalizing capital flowing from investors in industrial countries (now increasingly capital "service countries") has been guided by "cheap natural resources" and weak environmental regulation or enforcement in the global south, along with cheap labor.

Once again, this suggests that we should be extremely cautious in accepting arguments about "hypermaterialism" (superefficient technologies) as predicted by ecological modernization theorists (Mol and others). It is true that, for example, there has been some decoupling between energy consumption and increases in the gross national product (GNP) *within the United States* in the past two decades. Yet it is not true that all of the "U.S. GNP" arises from U.S. production. Much of the service revenues of U.S. *corporations* arise from coordinating investment and production *abroad*. When we examine the ecological impact of such non-U.S. production, we find increased materialism, with few limitations imposed by states or corporate entities on natural resource consumption (Goldman 1998; Sonnenfeld 2000). Returns on investment abroad add to the U.S. GNP, but ecological losses and natural resource consumption are not factored into the U.S. production record (York and Rosa 2003).

Transnationalizing the Treadmill

In its initial presentation, the treadmill was largely conceptualized as an analysis of the relationship of the U.S. political economy to the natural environment. Implications for other northern industrial economies were implicit, and the relationship of those economies to those of the global south was also alluded to. Nevertheless, it is clear that the treadmill itself already operated on a global scale and had significant global implications. *The Environment* (Schnaiberg 1980) was published just as:

- the nonaligned movement of southern nations was collapsing;
- the Washington Consensus on neoliberal global integration was gaining steam;
- transnational electronic networks were still under construction;
- southern debt crises were appearing on the horizon; and
- transnational trade liberalization agreements were yet to be fully negotiated.

As those changes to the global political economy emerged, the need for a more consciously transnational articulation of the treadmill model became clear.

The South Commission (1990) and the U.N. Conference on Environment and Development (the 1992 Earth Summit in Rio de Janeiro) both served to focus greater social attention on the global dimensions of environmental problems and the specific ways in which they were manifested in the global south. Highlighted was the relationship of the transnational economy to both growing global inequality and accelerating ecological degradation. As a result, in the first printing of *Environment and Society* in 1994, the treadmill was more deeply contextualized in global history and the transnational economy (Schnaiberg and Gould 2000). The global south was seen as moving from scarcity to even *greater* scarcity. The later iteration of the treadmill theory gave greater primacy to the northern industrial treadmill's historic and increasing reliance on access to the global south's natural resource pools, labor pools, markets, and waste sinks. So, too, were the implications of those transnational connections for domestic and international environmental *politics*.

Environment and Society emphasized the transnational distribution of economic benefits and ecological costs, and the acceleration of ecological withdrawals and additions. Also more clearly articulated were the resulting diminution of social returns to increased productive capacity and the structural dependency of labor. The focus was on economic actors with growing ease of transnational operation.[1] Although not welcomed as good news, our model of the transnationalization of the treadmill was well timed to meet the era of "globalization."

Environment and Society still predated important transnational events: the completion of the Uruguay Round of the General Agreement on Tariffs and Trade (GATT) negotiations; the establishment of the WTO; the ratification and implementation of NAFTA; and the resulting Zapatista rebellion in Chiapas, Mexico. It was also written before the full impacts of the collapse of the Eastern bloc Socialist economies could be assessed. Linkages between the transnational economy, the domestic treadmill, and local conflicts were more fully addressed in *Local Environmental Struggles* (Gould et al. 1996). That study overtly focused on transnational trade liberalization in the early post-NAFTA, and post-WTO, period. We noted the constraints these transnational institutions and processes placed on the trajectory of local conflicts as mediated through the national treadmill. The local scale at which most humans experience global dynamics was seen as increasingly shaped by changes imposed by globalization on national political economies.

Problematizing the then popular slogan of "Think globally, act locally," we argued that, because of the greater capacity of private capital actors to operate on a global scale, each locality was forced to compete with others because all were in an increasingly vulnerable competitive position. As a result, the effectiveness of local political action to protect the environment would be diminished, and environmental protection efforts would need to match the global scale of private capital actors. The local action valorized in much of the environmental sociology literature would thus be insufficient to alter the political economy in ways that would lead to a more sustainable development trajectory if that action was not networked and unified regionally, nationally, and transnationally.[2]

The growing hegemony of treadmill values and political economic forms manifest in corporate-led neoliberal globalization was further addressed in the new foreword to the Blackburn Press edition of *Environment and Society* in 2000 (Schnaiberg and Gould 2000). The brief introduction to the earlier work identified the treadmill model as a set of *global* processes, relations, and forces, decreasingly tied to the U.S. state. We noted that, in part because of the increasing power of transnational corporations vis-à-vis states, the treadmill had become more entrenched and less available to deceleration or dismantlement. Marking the twentieth anniversary of the publication of *The Environment,* the foreword articulated the extent to which the earliest national-level model had transnationalized and largely defeated competing alternative models for renegotiating socioenvironmental dynamics.

The foreword, however, also noted the emergence of new and/or renewed national and transnational political coalitions in opposition to a transnationalized treadmill. Most notably, by undermining the security of labor, treadmill transnationalization to some extent broke the alliance among workers, private capital, and the state that had been the primary engine of treadmill support (Rubin [1995] and others have called this the breaking of the "social contract" in U.S. labor relations). By simultaneously disempowering labor and accelerating ecological disruption, the transnational treadmill made it possible (or even necessary) for labor to lend support to the opponents of treadmill expansion at the *transnational* level. Labor-environmental coalitions in earlier iterations of treadmill theory emerged more at the dawn of the twenty-first century than they had in the 1980s (Gould et al. 2004). The transnationally organized "extralocal action" to confront the treadmill called for in *Local Environmental Struggles* finally emerged, especially in the anti-corporate globalization movement (Buttel and Gould 2004).

In short, as the scale of operation by treadmill actors increased through processes now termed *globalization,* the treadmill model scaled up to address the move from primarily national to primarily transnational political-economic arrangements. It did so without losing the analytical focus on and the centrality of national-level politics where transnational arrangements must be ratified or derailed. Nor did it lose sight of the implications of national and transnational forces at the local level, the level at which material social system–ecosystem interactions ultimately occur. The history of the past 28 years has provided ample empirical validation of the treadmill theory. A deepening commitment to treadmill expansion and less critical acceptance of treadmill values characterize this period. In addition, the period witnessed growing socioeconomic inequality, acceleration of the rate of ecosystem disorganization, and the failure of nonstructural regulatory efforts to reverse overall ecological decline as the state ceded more power to corporate interests.

Truck "reclaimed" by vegetation in the Cockscomb Basin Wildlife
Sanctuary, Belize, 2003. An Audubon Society information center now
occupies this location, a former Maya village site from which the Maya
were removed to protect jaguars. (photo by Ken Gould)

CHAPTER 5

Applying the Treadmill to Socioenvironmental Problems

1980–2008

Academic Responses to the Treadmill

Scholarly Evaluations

WHEN SCHNAIBERG PRESENTED the initial treadmill theory, it had no formal empirical evaluation. Indeed, the theory itself had been grounded by analytic induction (Glaser and Strauss 1967). In formal terms, this means that the theory "fit" the data from which it was actually abstracted. So the 1980 volume represented a grounded but untested theory. What has happened in the 1980–2008 period? Most directly, we have individually and collectively tested how well the treadmill *theory* explains the social production *trends* in the intervening decades. This includes work on Great Lakes water pollution (Gould 1991, 1992, 1994), on local mobilization for toxic waste control (Weinberg 1997), on local wetland protection efforts (Gould et al. 1996), on global environmental treaties (Gould et al. 1995; Gould et al. 1996), on the rise of postconsumer recycling in the United States (Weinberg et al. 2000), on ecotourism (Gould 1999), on local alternative technology initiatives in the global south (Schnaiberg and Gould 2000), and on environmental injustice in the waste

49

treatment and electronics industries (Pellow 2002; Pellow and Park 2002).

Each of these studies had a different set of specific questions, but all are subsumed under a general quest to determine whether recent social reforms have led to more socially progressive and ecologically sustainable production. While the details of each study differ, they all fail to find a substantial weakening or deceleration of the treadmill structures and processes. Indeed, as noted earlier, these studies were a painful lesson for us on how resilient the treadmill had become. To some extent, this resiliency has been fueled by the rise of profitability for U.S. corporations and the use of some of this financial windfall to capture political support through campaign contributions (Weinberg and Schnaiberg 2001). Paradoxically, the acceleration and globalization of the treadmill, as just noted, have also led to increasingly desperate efforts by state and local political officials seeking new investment to increase tax bases and employment opportunities. The result is a supply of treadmill-accelerating policies by the state and its corporate supporters, and a demand for accelerating the treadmill by displaced workers and their representatives.

The Treadmill of Production versus Ecological Modernization

It appears that there is more empirical (or political) support for the major contending theory—ecological modernization—that has emerged in the last decade or so (Beck 1992; Mol 1995). Central to ecological modernization theory is an assumption that the design, performance, and evaluation of production processes have been increasingly based on ecological as well as economic criteria (Mol 1995; Mol and Spaargaren 2000; Spaargaren 1997; Spaargaren and Mol 1992). As a theory of industrial change, ecological modernization suggests that we have entered a new industrial revolution, one of restructuring of production processes along ecological lines (Mol 1995). Yet recent summary and empirical critiques of ecological modernization theory (Schnaiberg et al. 2002; York and Rosa 2003) have indicated the methodological and theoretical limitations of such supporting studies. It is certainly true that the treadmill theory is insufficient to explain *all* patterns of economic and environmental change since 1980, but we believe that the evidence indicates stronger support for the treadmill model compared to the ecological modernization framework. While individual cases of ecological modernization have emerged in specific (and quite limited) sociopolitical contexts, the overall trend of the global production system is clearly toward ever-greater levels of ecological withdrawals and additions.

Especially in the absence of other major competing theories, the treadmill seems more congruent with recent history than any other theory at hand. And the treadmill theory is highly grounded in the processes of political-economic change in the United States, other industrial societies, and the south under globalization. Our argument is that the greater entrenchment of treadmill political-economic ideology and practices—that is, their *deeper* institutionalization in the global north and their greater *diffusion* across global trading systems—appears to be a continuing and, indeed, growing influence over actual environmental protection policies. And the best indicators seem to support this position. Generally speaking, despite their numerous successes, the environmental and environmental justice movements must confront the harsh reality that the political-economic structures on which this society operates have not been significantly altered with regard to ecological protection and social justice concerns.

In their evaluation of ecological modernization theory, York and Rosa (2003) compare the strength of that framework with political economic approaches to global environmental problems, including the treadmill of production model. Drawing on a range of examples (the Thai pulp industry, global environmental treaty ratification, the coal industry, the Dutch chemical industry, etc.), York and Rosa conclude that there is stronger evidence supporting the treadmill model than there is for ecological modernization. This is largely because the treadmill model actually evaluates more than the simple adoption of environmentally responsible policies. Scholars using the treadmill model examine whether it produces positive or negative ecological impacts locally and extralocally. Ecological modernization scholars have, on the whole, not pursued this line of analysis.

Hooks and Smith (2004) use the treadmill model to explain the relationship between Native American populations and hazardous munitions. They offer an innovative way of applying the tread-mill model to the literature of environmental justice. In addition, they envision the U.S. military-industrial complex as a treadmill institution, but driven primarily by *geopolitical* and *social/racial* motives rather than by industrial-capitalist influences (as treadmill scholars suggest). They argue that treadmill scholars have not focused enough on the phenomena of militarism, violence, and co-ercion in U.S. environmental politics and history (although Gould [2007] has done some recent work on this). This position offers a useful bridge between the emphasis on class conflict of the tread-mill state and the ethnocentric and racist politics of the military state. Hooks and Smith also argue that treadmill institutions oper-ate with much greater autonomy than the treadmill model may allow for. The works of Hooks and Smith (2004), Gedicks (2001), and Homer-Dixon (2001) suggest ways in which militarism, vio-lence, and physical coercion may be more fully incorporated into treadmill analyses.

What Forces Have Limited the Diffusion of the Treadmill in Environmental Sociology?

Northern Environmental Analysts

Just a few months after the publication of *The Environment: From Surplus to Scarcity,* Ronald Reagan was elected president of the United States. He ushered in a neoconservative agenda, emphasiz-ing state deregulation and transnational neoliberalism. This new political zeitgeist of the 1980s was clearly antithetical to the tread-mill theory's articulation of the need for "politics over markets" (Lindblom 1977). The antienvironmental, treadmill-accelerating agenda simultaneously validated the treadmill model while making resistance to the treadmill more difficult. By increasing the power and liberty of transnational corporations and treadmill elites, roll-ing back the initial gains of environmentalists, and launching an attack on the countervailing forces that had sought to constrain cor-porate power (Derber 1998), the Reagan administration dimmed the prospects for slowing or dismantling the treadmill just as the theoretical framework was making its intellectual debut.

The declining power of organized labor, which had been a powerful force promoting both progressive distribution and environmental health, had some impact as well. The civil resistance begun in the 1960s and 1970s (Shuman 1998), which offered countervailing forces to the treadmill of production, also waned. Environmental and other social movements, which were often insurgent prior to the publication of *The Environment*, became more conservative. They became more cooperative with those controlling private capital and the state. Adoption of "Third Wave" environmentalism strategies supplanted earlier insurgence (Dowie 1995). An increasingly professional, mainstream environmental movement now emphasized cooperative approaches; voluntary action on the part of treadmill actors; and "flexible," market-based approaches to source reduction and ecosystem protection. This stance resonated well with the Reagan administration's neoliberal political-economic agenda (and continued into the Clinton and Bush eras), but it withdrew any serious challenges to the treadmill.

Southern Environmental Analysts

Transnationally, the southern debt crises of the 1980s disabled many alternative development strategies adopted by developing nations and crushed most alternative treadmill pilot projects. The weight of international debt payments and the international financial institutions' structural adjustment policies suppressed efforts to build alternative structures for production and distribution. Ideological support for such efforts from the "mixed economies" and social welfare states of Europe diminished as well. The combined influence of Reagan in the United States and Thatcher in the United Kingdom shifted the global political climate and also led to an upsurge in U.S. military interventions and muscle flexing around the globe (Blum 1995). Transnational insurgence against the Washington Consensus model of global economic integration was displaced by new corporate libertarian deregulatory regimes (Derber 1998; Korten 2001). Dismantlement of the state socialist economies of the Eastern bloc at the start of the 1990s and their replacement with "shock therapy" policies of Western "free markets" removed the last global social support for opposition to the treadmill. The treadmill emerged as the only path for social and economic change, regardless of its ecological consequences.[1]

All of those changes to domestic and transnational political economies, and the resultant acceleration of ecological disorganization, poverty, and inequality, served to validate empirically the predictions of the treadmill model. Yet, even as the treadmill theory proved correct in assessing the causes, consequences, and necessary alternatives to ecological degradation, it became less viable politically.

Tensions Affecting Northern Environmental Sociologists

Those seeking to further their careers in the study of socio-environmental dynamics were thus deterred from adopting a theoretical framework that lay in direct opposition to the policy regimes of the state, private capital, and international financial institutions. A better option was to search for models that might be more amenable to the political and economic zeitgeist. Mainstream environmental *movements* had chosen to move toward Third Wave environmentalism, and their influence on the *field* of environmental sociology should not be underestimated. With radical, structural, proenvironmental change off the political agenda, some environmental scholars retreated into intellectual abstraction.

They sought insights and careers in constructionist models. These posed no threat or challenge to power holders, who controlled access to grant funding and policy makers. Other scholars chose to focus on areas of apparent environmentalist success in an era of major environmentalist failure. They chose to reify grassroots struggles as national and transnational struggles failed. Others chose to adapt Third Wave environmentalism into sociological theory. In this view, the treadmill would simply self-correct for environmental limits through market mechanisms. These strategies supported, rather than opposed, the emerging neoliberal agenda.[2]

Additionally, some of the resistance to the treadmill model stems from its power to nullify commonly proposed and often popular, nonstructural solutions to environmental problems (i.e., efficiency, recycling, appropriate technology, ecological modernization, ecotourism, population control, attitude adjustment, voluntary simplicity, etc.). Many of these solutions had become sacred cows of the environmental movement when *The Environment* was published, thus providing a political opening to cast the treadmill theory simultaneously as anticapitalist *and* antienvironmentalist. By presenting structurally based critiques of the solutions offered by both treadmill elites and their environmentalist opponents, the theoretical framework was left with few potential political and intellectual allies. Even those within the academy critique the treadmill model more often as "depressing" than inaccurate, reflecting the model's utility in debunking the environmental myths surrounding nonstructural paths to socioecologically sustainable development trajectories.

Environment and Society: The Enduring Conflict (Schnaiberg and Gould 2000) included critical analyses of recycling and "appropriate technology," and called more overtly for political conflict. This position served to deepen the alienation of both treadmill elites and mainstream environmentalists from treadmill theory. Many environmentalists, and perhaps environmental sociologists, sought environmentalism as a means to make an end run around the deeply structural and especially distributional questions at the heart of politics since the dawn of the Industrial Revolution (as evidenced in slogans such as, "not left or right, but forward") and thus sought to avoid difficult political conflicts and confrontations. The treadmill's implication that political conflict and distributional issues would have to be at the heart of any viable attempt to establish an ecologically sustainable order was, however, simply distasteful to the sensibilities and fonder hopes of many of those to whom the environment was a central concern.

Mainstream versus Minority Analysts in the North

The treadmill model does imply the need for major structural changes—indeed, some would argue revolutionary changes are needed to create socioecological sustainability in the transnational system. The model locates solutions largely in macrostructural domains that are not as clearly and overtly "environmental" as those that attracted many environmental sociologists (as well as many environmental activists) to the field. It implies that much of the research of environmental sociologists may be irrelevant, or only tangentially useful, to resolving environmental crises.

This limitation helps explain the scholarly hiatus between a professional American Sociological Association section, often intent on establishing a new professional domain, and the societal need to integrate ecological factors in political and economic world systems, labor, race and ethnicity, and other interest areas within the discipline. Economic elite-state relations, information control, and control of science and technology research and development already had preestablished professional social scientific stakeholders. Those stakeholders had macrostructural concerns motivating their research, and environmental issues could only be *added* to these agendas but could not *displace* them. From a treadmill perspective, there may be less intellectual justification for *environmental* sociologists to examine economic policy, in which *environmental policy* is intrinsically embedded. Likewise, *environmental* sociologists have less claim to study all antisystemic movements, whose support is required by *environmental* movements to effect change, or to study technology policy generally as opposed to *Green technology* initiatives.

Most "reasonable" scholars have taken revolutionary or even macrostructural change to the political economy off the table, as either highly unlikely or impossible. They may be correct. In that context, the treadmill implies that the dream of solving environmental crises and achieving "sustainable development" is unlikely or impossible (and is thus an *Enduring Conflict*).[3] As nonstructural solutions fail, however, the value of treadmill theory, with all of its unpleasant implications and difficult challenges, may slowly emerge as compelling. Deepening ecological disorganization, declining social returns on treadmill-dominated development, and disillusion with alternative theoretical frameworks may lead to a resurgence of interest in treadmill theory. A generation of younger U.S. scholars may be willing to accept the conflict and difficulty borne of earlier political and intellectual failures (partly stemming from the politically naive and overly idealistic expectations of environmentalists of the 1960s and 1970s). Across the globe, emergence of transnational resistance to the transnational treadmill at various levels and in various forms may further fuel such a shift in orientation.[4]

Have Environmental Movements in the United States or Elsewhere Adopted the Treadmill Theory?

Resistance from Environmental Movements in the North

It is unfortunate that the treadmill model has not been widely adopted by mainstream environmental social movements. Adoption might have led environmental organizations to serve as a countervailing force. They would then more likely oppose the increasing power of corporate polluters and reduced state intervention in economic markets. Much of U.S. mainstream environmentalism actually moved toward the adoption of *protreadmill* values in the 1980s and 1990s as a means to preserve their access to policy makers, to permit more cooperative relations with major polluters, and to gain greater access to funding from foundations and wealthy private donors (Dowie 1995; Gonzalez 2001). Among the reasons for this movement, we note the diffusion of the following political-economic ideologies:

- the growing hegemony of neoliberal "free-market" ideology domestically ("Reaganomics");
- similar ideologies in Western European mixed economies ("Thatcherism");
- equivalent theories in Eastern Europe and the former Soviet Union (shock therapy); and
- parallel policies in the global south (structural adjustment).

All of these ideologies appeared to take any alternative model of development off the table. A domestic and transnational political milieu was created, which produced institutionalized political resistance to critical treadmill-related ideas. Cooperation with treadmill institutions was a means to gain whatever environmental protection might be acceptable to economic and political leaders (Athanasiou 1996). Immediate gains (even if minor, ephemeral, and offset by more significant losses) are important to social movement organizations. They depend on expanding their "postal" memberships to demonstrate their effectiveness, thereby also enhancing external funding because of the size of their constituency.

Mainstream environmental organizations often share board members with transnational corporations (Brulle 2000). They also frequently share class (and race and gender) status. The treadmill model's emphasis on structured class interests, distributional dimensions, and emergent conflicts thus lacked appeal. Leadership, membership, and funding constituencies were thus firmly rooted in class and race privilege. As one environmental justice activist recently stated to us, "The leaders of the mainstream environmental movement are the sons and daughters of the industrialists producing much of the world's pollution."

Additionally, the core environmentalist constituency that emerged from the political turmoil of the 1960s and 1970s in the United States was not inclined toward political conflict and direct confrontation with power holders (Mitchell 1980). Other social movements of that era were much more explicitly conflictual. Environmentalism necessitated *some* opposition to elites but never encouraged a real structural critique of socioeconomic conditions. This contrasted with New Left, anti-imperialist, and even civil rights movements. Costs and benefits of environmental degradation and environmental destruction were largely viewed as a *shared* burden and benefit (especially when filtered through a *survivalist* frame, both in the late 1960s and in the later rise of *global* concerns). Environmental activists with more structural ideologies and approaches were drawn mostly from *other* movements that focused less on ecological problems as a key issue.

Class-Based Northern Movements That Share the Treadmill Perspective

Initially, the presentation of the treadmill model did not overtly address racial inequality. Thus, when civil rights movements incorporated environmental factors as a significant part of racial inequality in their emerging *environmental justice* movement, they largely ignored the treadmill framework. Although the people-of-color environmental justice movement is firmly rooted in the distributional dimensions of environmental degradation, the American intellectual and political milieu that routinely frames race and class dimensions of inequality as oppositional rather than synergistic, made it difficult for that movement to immediately gravitate toward a model that places class-based inequality centrally in the analysis (see the next section).[5]

In contrast, the *antitoxics* movement of the citizen-worker (white, working class) came closer to adopting the treadmill framework. This movement acknowledged both the diminishing returns to the working class produced by loyalty to the treadmill forces and a growing awareness of environmental health costs. The movement's members articulated a more class-based opposition to business as usual (Stretton 1976), grasping the growing environmental health risks and the decreasing number of jobs and job security offered by treadmill producers. Hence, they *implicitly* accepted many of the basic premises of the treadmill theory and coupled this acceptance with a working-class tradition of union organizing and direct confrontation of power holders. Echoing community organizers such as Saul Alinsky, antitoxics leader Lois Gibbs often declared, "There are two kinds of people: those with power and those without power who must take it back." While the civil rights movement had produced a similar legacy of political confrontation that undergirded the environmental justice movement, it lacked a direct link to treadmill theory (see the next section). The antitoxics movement advanced from local concerns toward a more universal ideology articulated in Lois Gibbs's famous "plugging up the toilets" strategy for forcing structural reform (Szasz 1994). At this juncture, the antitoxics movement and treadmill theory became somewhat more convergent.[6]

Southern and Global Social Movements' Resonance with the Treadmill

The four books that articulated treadmill theory have been unavailable in the primary languages of the global south (especially Spanish). The model appears, however, to have resonance with the environmental livelihood struggles in peripheral nations of the global economy. *Environment and Society* offered a more transnational set of forces and processes applicable to the south and thus found an audience among academic activists and intellectuals that was positively disposed.

Scholar-activism and "public sociology" are more the norm than the exception in the south (especially in Latin America), in contrast to their status as an aberration in the north. Hence, the dissemination of treadmill theory among environmental scholars in the south in the 1990s provided a route for transmission of the model to southern environmental movements. Compared with scholars in the north, those in the south are more likely to view the practice of "speaking truth to power" in their writing, teaching, and service work as an obligation rather than a burden shouldered by a few academics. This is so despite greater potential risks to their careers and personal security.

Macrostructural analysis, issues of distribution, and unequal power relations are central topics of popular as well as academic discourse in much of the south. Thus, the treadmill theory, which has strong resonance with dependency theory and world-systems theory in its 1990's articulations, may have found a more receptive audience in the south than in the United States (see Gould 2003, 2006).

Southern environmentalism integrated ecological and social systems, viewing environmental and livelihood struggles as inseparable when place, production, and identity politics converge (Gould 1999).[7] This fusion gave treadmill-based critiques more resonance there. Rejected were northern mainstream environmental movements' arguments rooted in population and culture.[8] Southern convergence of environmental, identity, and production struggles may be widely shared by the transnational anti–corporate globalization movement. That social movement has most clearly adopted treadmill analytical frameworks in formulating an ideology of opposition to corporate power, market mechanisms, and international financial institutions (Buttel and Gould 2004). The anti–corporate globalization movement forms a complex coalition of coalitions. It incorporates a focus on macrostructural processes, corporate power, inequality, and the environment. Additionally, it believes in the necessity of political confrontation of power holders (corporations, international financial institutions, and state elites) to produce both better distribution of the benefits of production and greater protection of the ecological bases of quality of life issues. And these strategies resonate powerfully with the path toward treadmill deceleration and/or dismantlement articulated in our works. This movement has produced a series of highly sophisticated structural critiques[9] with direct references to treadmill theory, which indicates that the treadmill model may have its greatest overt influence in anti-corporate globalization circles.

Anti-corporate globalization movements represent a convergence of organized labor, human rights, social justice, indigenous rights, women's rights, and southern environmental movements (among others) (Gould et al. 2004). Central in their programs are the search for distributional and environmental gains through macrostructural reorganization and a radical democratization of power. This movement brings together disparate constituencies, all of whom tend to be relatively positively disposed toward treadmill-style analyses. These constituencies include:

- southern environmentalists,
- disenfranchised labor,
- some northern environmentalists, and
- southern and northern environmental justice advocates,
- advocates from multiple racial/ethnic populations.

Because of the analytical orientations of its coalition components, the anti-corporate globalization movement is structurally inclined, politically confrontational, and deeply concerned with environmental and social justice (Buttel and Gould 2004).[10]

PART III

The Future Role of the Treadmill Theory

The Champion Paper Mill on the Pigeon River in Canton, North Carolina, 1997. Dioxin contamination from the mill has been blamed for numerous deaths and illnesses downriver in Tennessee. (photo by Ken Gould)

CHAPTER **6**

Is the Treadmill More/ Still Useful Today for Ecological Analyses? for Social Analyses?

MORE AND MORE, younger scholars are drawing on the treadmill because of the pain of their discovery of widening social inequalities and ecological decline. The treadmill model offers both a description of antisocial and antiecological tendencies within the global economy, *and* a richer, more reflective analysis of what changes may be brought about by analysts and activists. Perhaps national and global environmental politics support and reflect the treadmill model more than they do other theoretical frameworks. New alignments of workers, community movements, and labor unions are built around a shared sense of the pernicious impact of the treadmill on the majority of workers in many countries.

Conflicts over environmental protection have recently become more contentious, more transnational, and more multifaceted. The "Battle in Seattle" at the World Trade Organization's millennium round of talks, recurring protests at meetings of the World Bank and International Monetary Fund (IMF), street battles surrounding Free Trade Area of the Americas (FTAA) negotiations, and the shutdown of talks at the WTO meeting in Cancun attest to this. Environmental protection is no longer restricted to the domain of policy "experts," academics, and scientists. People are starving, while land and watersheds, forests, and ways of life are being destroyed (Gedicks 2001; Goldman 1998).

Scholars need frameworks and models that reflect stakeholders' realities. The treadmill has always offered this, particularly for academics willing to accept the possibility that the trajectory of national and global environmental protection has been limited at best. Abstract, detached modeling techniques and opaque theoretical constructions are not as accessible, useful, or appealing to scholars, students, and the public who seek to understand this contentious and ecologically disorganized world. After more than three decades of institutionalized environmental protection at the U.S. federal level, why is the United States more ecologically compromised than ever before?[1]

Additionally, the treadmill offers a much more credible and useful theoretical link between environmental sociology and other subfields within the sociological discipline. While environmental sociology claims to be *interdisciplinary* (Dunlap and Michelson 2002), its weaknesses include its failure to build lasting bridges to *sociology* itself. The treadmill of production bridges environmental sociology with the sociology of work; the sociology of labor; Marxist sociology; political sociology; urban sociology; the sociology of the world system; and the sociology of race, gender, and class.

Equally important is the capacity of treadmill scholars to speak to all sociologists. This affords the latter a broader scope to incorporate environmental factors into their epistemological, methodological, and theoretical work. Nonenvironmental sociologists might deepen and broaden their approaches to sociological phenomena by adopting what Buttel and Humphrey (2002) term the "double determination"—an approach to the study of society that incorporates both *social* theory and a focus on the *natural* world or ecosystems. Treadmill scholars have always understood that environmental politics are driven by both social/human and ecological/natural factors and limitations. Environmental sociology's founders intended to challenge the dominant Durkheimian paradigm, which restricted sociologists to explaining social phenomena only through reference to other social phenomena (thus ignoring the interactions between human societies and ecosystems). A broadening of this approach is intrinsic in treadmill analyses.

The Treadmill of Production and Environmental Justice

Another key theoretical contribution is the link between the treadmill model and more recent developments in environmental sociology. For example, the treadmill of production predated the now well-established field of environmental justice studies and advanced the argument that environmental problems and solutions are not shared equally across or within populations. It laid a foundation for more recent research that has focused on how other forms of inequality (such as race and gender) intersect with environmental policy. Schnaiberg's 1980 work is prominently cited in many environmental justice studies and texts, including Robert Bullard's landmark book *Dumping in Dixie* (1990) (see also Hurley 1995; Pellow 2002; Pellow and Park 2002; Walsh et al. 1997). However, many environmental justice scholars have not paid adequate attention to the treadmill of production. In the following sections, we consider where environmental justice studies have fallen short of their ambitious intellectual and political mark.

Class versus Race and the Treadmill

As environmental justice scholars reflect on the impact of two decades of activism, critical questions are emerging. Pellow and Brulle (2005) discuss the *race-versus-class* divide in both the environmental justice movement and in scholarly circles. The question partly arises from the recognition that many environmental justice scholars have yet to integrate the treadmill into their own research framework. The race-versus-class debate in the environmental justice literature (whether the strongest predictor of where toxic facilities should be located is the race or class composition of the host community) has raged since the release of the United

Church of Christ's report *Toxic Wastes and Race in the U.S.* (1987). Recent research has produced interesting methodological advances in the study of environmental racism/inequality, but it often misses the structural framework that the treadmill offers. Researchers argue over whether zip codes or census tracts are the most appropriate level of analysis for environmental justice studies, while communities continue to be inundated with pollution. Environmental injustice has always been about *both* race and class; yet most scholars have missed this point (for an example of a study that successfully integrates both dimensions, see Faber and Krieg 2001). The environmental justice movement has had to work hard to claim ownership over the discourse and the politics of environmental inequity that is centered in communities of color where environmental injustice is evident. Thus, the discourse, ideology, and framing of the problem of environmental justice have focused heavily on environmental *racism,* often without fully examining the class bases of environmental inequality (Gandall 2007; Gould 2006). But many environmental justice conflicts in communities of color simply cannot be explained by racism alone. Some examples of this follow:

- Operation Silver Shovel was a scandal in Chicago during the mid-1990s, wherein tons of construction waste were illegally dumped in Latino and African American neighborhoods. The culprits: white-owned construction companies, waste dumpers, and the Latino and African American politicians who accepted bribes to look the other way (Pellow 2002).
- On numerous Native American reservations, tribal leaders have accepted payment to allow nuclear waste and other locally unwanted land uses (LULUs) to be sited, over objections of tribal members (LaDuke 1999).
- In the home-based, high-tech toxic sweatshops of Silicon Valley, we find that Vietnamese immigrant entrepreneurs exploit members of their own ethnic group in the name of profit and the American Dream (Pellow and Park 2002).

Each of these cases reflects the ways in which treadmill institutions engage in both environmental racism and environmental classism/inequality. Thus, the treadmill model has critical theoretical importance for environmental justice studies.

Globalization, Environmental Injustice, and the Treadmill

Studies using the treadmill of production model revealed the transnational nature of corporate and state power (through economic globalization and free trade) and their links to the globalization of environmental hazards. Environmental justice studies, on the other hand, have only recently begun to explore this dynamic (Adeola 2000; Agyeman et al. 2003; Taylor 1995; Westra and Lawson 2001). While it is true that international financial institutions and global markets have facilitated the global mobility of capital from north to south, there is another factor that we should not lose sight of.

Specifically, the environmental and environmental justice movements in the north have unwittingly contributed (at least partially) to the flow of destructive multinational capital operations and hazardous wastes to the south.[2] This shift in polluting technologies and "development" has affected not only the ecosystem but also public health all around the globe, especially on indigenous lands. "Ironically, the development of a North American environmental justice movement, which provided for greater environmental protection and greater citizen involvement in the permitting process, contributed to an intensified assault against native peoples in the Third World" (Gedicks 2001: 197).

A small number of scholars, journalists, and activists are paying attention to this problematic outcome of the mobilization of social movements in the north, but those numbers are few and far between (Hilz 1992: 43; Moyers 1990: 3–7; Palmer 2005). There are two stories here. The first is a cautionary tale that movements in the north should be more careful about how they approach the problem of pollution in the region, given the realities of globalization. The second story is much more hopeful because it reveals that social movements *do* have real power to impact corporate and state decision making. The real difficulty is devising ways to guide that power to yield more progressive consequences.

Burdens and Benefits

While so much of the research on environmental injustice has focused on the burdens of the treadmill of production, few scholars have emphasized the attendant *benefits* that accrue to communities that are *not* confronting such hazards (Bullard 2004; Gould 2006). We have scores of studies of reservations, barrios, ghettoes, Chinatowns, and poor/working-class urban and rural communities across the United States that are inundated with environmental harm (burdens); yet we have next to no studies of wealthy, environmentally protected, socially privileged communities. This is a fundamental gap in the literature that studies of the treadmill of production could address because treadmill-of-production scholars have typically emphasized both sides of this question. Sociologists understand that social inequality is relational. Environmental racism and class inequalities affect populations in a *relational* fashion. That is, one group's access to clean living and/or working environments is often made possible by the restriction of another group's access to those same amenities.

For example, while residents in communities of color battle industry, city hall, and the courts over decent-paying, safe jobs and locally unwanted land uses, white, middle-class and affluent populations have jobs and live in communities that are the most ecologically protected (Pulido 2000, Gould 2006). There is a limited supply of ecologically desirable space and jobs in urban areas. White, middle-class residents and decision makers possess a greater capability than do people of color and low-income residents to secure these valued spaces and do so, effectively restricting access to these goods. The following are a few brief examples.

- A metal plating facility that was responsible for polluting an immigrant Latino neighborhood in San Diego, California, for years was owned by a man who lived in the wealthy, beautiful coastal community of La Jolla (home to an ecological preserve where all marine life is protected by law). When environmental health and justice activists finally succeeded in shutting down the metal plating facility, the community was left to seek compensatory economic development, while the owner could simply invest in another financial venture in another desperate neighborhood anywhere in the world. The two communities remained relatively the same: one economically depressed and heavily polluted, the other economically privileged and relatively unpolluted.

• In December 1997, a number of residents of Chicago's African American community of Austin employed by a North Side remodeling company were cited for illegally dumping debris in their own community. "You have companies and residents, bringing garbage from the suburbs back into their own neighborhoods," one observer commented (McNeil 1998). This practice was compounded by Operation Silver Shovel (mentioned in an earlier section), the illegal dumping of construction and demolition debris in these same communities. The result was that suburban, middle-class, mostly Anglo communities received the spatial, environmental, and economic benefits of new transportation corridors, gentrification, and urban sprawl, while this desperately poor African American neighborhood was burdened with the leftover waste products of that development.

• Aspen, Colorado, is a popular vacation spot for middle-class and wealthy tourists. It is also a place where millionaires and billionaires own second and third homes whose average price is nearly $4 million (as of 2004). Aspen prides itself on its reputation as an environmentally sustainable municipality, surrounded by the natural beauty of the Colorado Rocky Mountains and clean river water. Aspen is home to numerous environmental organizations and think tanks focused on ecological sustainability. Some public officials believe that one key to maintaining a sustainable environment is by limiting immigration to the United States. The city council recently passed a resolution promoting stronger national immigration controls to maintain population stabilization in the United States and discourage migrants from crossing the United States–Mexican border to work and live here. Yet many of these migrants work in the tourism,

hotel, construction, landscaping, and food service industries that form the basis of Aspen's survival and the town's
appeal to the wealthy. Moreover, many of the (part-time
and full-time) wealthy residents have made their fortunes
from investing in global markets that have likely wreaked
ecological and social havoc in various places around the
world. Yet the global investment activities of the rich in
Aspen remain invisible.

Each of the examples just cited demonstrates the ways that
the costs and the benefits of environmental injustice are un-
evenly distributed and the ways that both are less visible to the
public.

Perhaps one way to underscore these inequalities is to increase
the costs and the risks of environmental inequality for elites
(Gould 2006). For example, many global environmental justice
activists have sought to return toxic waste dumped in the global
south to its nation of origin. Incredibly, as a result of years of
campaigning, this has recently happened (e.g., mercury dumped
in India was returned to Europe, and municipal incinerator waste
dumped in Haiti was returned to Philadelphia). There are similar ongoing campaigns in Mozambique, South Africa, and many
other southern nations. If the producers of such wastes—the
beneficiaries of environmental injustices—were no longer allowed
to remain anonymous and escape the consequences of their actions, the underlying power dynamic producing environmental
inequalities might be challenged.

Picking the Right Targets

The last point that we will make regarding environmental
justice studies and the treadmill is the overemphasis on environmental policy making to the neglect of the more deeply
rooted problems of class domination and institutional racism
that allow capitalism to thrive. While it is certainly logical to
target those institutions making environmental policy in this
nation, Gould (2006) points out that eliminating environmental
racism would alleviate only a portion of the problem because
racial discrimination pervades all American institutions and

racism in education, labor and housing markets, and elsewhere would continue. Racism and class inequality together create forces of oppression and barriers to environmental justice that should reveal to critical scholars and activists one conclusion: environmental justice is fundamentally incompatible with the logic of capitalism (see Benford 2005; Gould 2006). Or, conversely, environmental *in*justice is a normal consequence of the way capitalist/market economies function. That is, the treadmill of production produces widespread social and environmental inequalities as a matter of course. Pathologically, a sign of capitalism's health and robustness is how poorly the working classes and ecosystems are faring. Unlike most environmental sociologists and environmental justice scholars, we have no hesitation reaching this logical conclusion, which virtually all environmental justice studies implicitly support.

Thus, in such a system, poor people and people of color encounter "multiple jeopardies" (Collins 2000) because they enjoy few of the benefits of the economic system *and* endure its associated environmental harms. Changing this system would require enduring, disruptive, and sustained political conflict, which would involve collaboration between the poor/lower/ working and middle classes (Gould 2006; Schnaiberg and Gould 2000). Clarke (1996) argues that even before we can talk of a long-term vision of sustainability and social justice, we must reclaim "popular sovereignty"—those basic rights such as access to food, water, education, health care, and a clean environment, all of which have been codified in various international conventions, yet all but ignored by many nation-states and transnational corporations. Revival and recognition of these rights would, in itself, constitute a repudiation of capitalism and a discursive call for revolution.

Choosing the right targets also means broadening our understanding of politics and the political opportunity structure beyond the state (Tilly 1978) to include the power of private capital and its ongoing impact on governance (Pellow 2001). As a South African environmental justice activist told us recently, "One of our primary goals is to weaken the power of corporations over the state, because for too long they have had an enormous influence over government policy making." Activists around the world are making the same point and focusing their energies on corporate-state alliances that continue to produce "low road to development" (Harrison 1994) models, free trade agreements, and environmental inequalities on all geographic scales. Scholars of social movements and environmental justice have yet to theorize about the profound impact of growing transnational private capital on states around the globe. The treadmill of production model provided a foundation for this kind of thinking more than two decades ago (Schnaiberg 1980) and refined itself over the years (Schnaiberg 1994; Schnaiberg and Gould 2000; Gould, et al. 1996).

The treadmill is therefore particularly useful today for ecological and social analyses. Scholars engaged in critical analyses of various environmental issues or social issues with environmental implications can draw on the logic of the treadmill of production to facilitate more robust, credible sociological research. For example, numerous scholars and observers view much of postapartheid South Africa as a model for other nations seeking to confront racism and thorny questions of social justice and reparations. This may be warranted on some narrow plane. Despite the official fall of a racist government, however, the problems of environmental racism and injustice have only worsened since 1994. The reason is simple: in an effort to adopt a neoliberal economic agenda (free markets, job growth, increasing gross domestic product [GDP], etc.), the South African government, under the presidency of Nelson Mandela and since then, actively sought to increase corporate investment from around the globe. Not surprisingly, this campaign resulted in many heavily polluting industries locating or expanding in that nation, many of which are in close proximity to neighborhoods and lands on which black South Africans were forced to live under the apartheid era. To be fair, environmental racism was already a hallmark of apartheid. The postapartheid agenda worsened the situation, however, despite the official democratization of South Africa. As oil refineries, hazardous waste incinerators, landfills, and a host of other locally unwanted land uses are proliferating around South Africa, nearby residents and workers are contracting cancer and a range of environmental illnesses (McDonald 2002). Predictably, this state of affairs is viewed positively by international financial institutions, transnational corporations, and the corporate-controlled media as evidence that South Africa has entered the modern age. An analysis of this situation that draws on the treadmill of production would have predicted this outcome as early as 1994.

A clear-cut landscape on Vancouver Island, British Columbia, 1994. Conflicts between environmentalists, logging interests, and aboriginal peoples raged through the 1990s over the fate of areas such as Clayoquot Sound. (photo by Ken Gould)

CHAPTER 7

What Are the Implications of the Treadmill for the Potential Attainment of Socially and Ecologically Sustainable Development Trajectories?

WE EACH HAVE EVOLVED somewhat different political assessments of what is to be done in the face of the history of the treadmill.[1] In part this is because of the complex conditions that have helped expand the treadmill. While we share similar *scientific* evaluations of what has gone wrong in the globalizing treadmill, each of us has a somewhat different *political judgment* about what parts of this system are amenable to change.

One position is that more structural reforms need to be implemented through the existing political system of the United States and other major industrial societies. The major mechanism that will induce or coerce such change will be an increasing mobilization of those discontented with the social and ecological impacts of the treadmill. In addition to traditional environmentalists, conservationists, and preservationists, a second major component of a potential coalition is that of environmental justice and antienvironmental racism organizations (see chapter 6). Labor organizations, which have been both beneficiaries and casualties of the acceleration of the treadmill, have to become a coalition partner if a coalition is to be taken seriously by both political representatives and corporate elites. Organized labor's relations with many environmental organizations and social justice organizations have been episodic and conflicted (Gould et al. 2005; Obach 2004).

A few state policies have incorporated elements of all three interests: environmental, environmental justice, and labor. President Clinton signed an executive order to incorporate environmental justice evaluations of federal programs. But the actual implementation and force of these evaluations have been problematic. In much the same way, the National Environmental Policy Act's (NEPA) (1969) requirements for environmental impact assessments have always been highly circumscribed (Schnaiberg 1980; Gould 1988). Implementation of international Great Lakes water pollution standards were similarly undermined by corporate and community concerns (Gould 1991). Likewise, the stringent toxic waste reporting requirements of RCRA (1976) that incorporated the "community right-to-know" provisions have been undermined since the act's early implementation (Weinberg 1997). Protection of workers from occupational hazards has also been continuously challenged by employers, both public and private (Pellow 2002).

For some time, we have observed the growing displacement of middle-class educated workers (Gould et al. 1996; Krugman 2003; Leicht and Fitzgerald 2007). This stratum could offer some organizational capacity to merge some of the disparate concerns of a potential socioenvironmental coalition. Perhaps the most limiting condition for the rise of any such coalescence has been the absence of an alternative production system to the treadmill. Such a coalition ultimately lacks the capacity to mobilize private and public capital and to open up new organizations of work, natural resource use, and political representation of both labor and environmental concerns.

In contrast to the enduring, conflicting aspects of the treadmill, there is an attraction to the comforting expectations of reflexive modernization, as argued in the ecological modernization theory. Yet these seem equally improbable to generate a successful production revolution in the near term. Whenever a more economically conservative U.S. administration has taken control, for example, state environmental protection diminishes and political support for more rapid technological change is enhanced (especially noteworthy in the Bush regime). This raises the need for a more enduring, mobilized coalition of opposition to the expansion of the treadmill as the major political-economic strategy of the society. Yet as we have noted, these models are less available in a post-Soviet period.

Ultimately, the treadmill is simultaneously a disappointing and uplifting narrative. It dispels any belief that the state of global environmental protection is tolerable, and it makes clear what the driving forces behind these remaining problems are. For those stakeholders who wish to move toward a socially just and ecologically sustainable future, the treadmill disabuses us of the notion that someone else will take care of the problem or that reaching a solution will be easy. The root of the problem, the treadmill theory notes, is the power of elite institutions to construct reality and define the environmental situation for the mass public, while exercising extraordinary material and structural power over both people and ecosystems (Beder 1997). Activists have, in recent years, become much more aware of the problematic alliance between corporations and the state and how this alliance has deeply negative implications for environmental protection in particular and for democratic governance in general (Mander and Goldsmith 1996; Pellow 2002).[2]

Another enduring hallmark of treadmill institutions is the willingness of elites within them to use violence, coercion, and repression to achieve their ends. Virtually every WTO, World Bank, and IMF meeting since 1999 has witnessed peaceful demonstrations by activists being disrupted by violent state repression. In the face of such power and abuse, citizen-workers have to be prepared to respond to, diffuse, deflect, and challenge such elite tactics. One certainty is that both more radical action and a more radical vision are required to decelerate the treadmill, in contrast to the perspective of the mainstream environmental movement. There is an overarching need to attain democratic forms of governance and to rethink and transform our basic ideas about the *social* purpose of business, development, and work (Korten 2001).[3]

All social movements must combine theory with action, or diagnostic frames with tactics. The treadmill presents activists with a useful theory that gets at the core of critical questions, including why environmental protection efforts have failed; why corporations have become so hegemonic; why workers and environmentalists will not be able to form productive alliances without a great deal of effort; and why radical action is necessary to challenge these problems. The most important thing about changing the world is to know what is wrong with it in the first place (i.e., a diagnostic frame), and the treadmill makes this quite clear. As to how activists and others might take this analysis into the tactical frame arena, we leave that up to them.

The Failures of Nonstructural Change

At its most basic level, the treadmill model argues that traditionally accepted and promoted mechanisms of achieving environmental protection will fall short, as they fail to account for the antiecological logic of capital. We have sought Green technology, greater efficiency, cooperative agreements with private capital interests, market mechanisms for pollution control, voluntary simplicity, and related policy tinkering. Yet all essentially fail to adequately account for the macrostructural constraints and incentives embedded in domestic and transnational political economies. They also ignore the central role played by *social inequality* in generating both treadmill support and ecological decline.

Most of the claims for the value of Green technology fail to address power relations in the control of scientific and technological research and development (Schnaiberg 1977). In theory, Green technologies could reduce the rate of ecological disorganization. Such a radical redirection of technology is not likely to occur, however. Structured incentives for the large private capital interests that fund, organize, and direct technological innovation will remain unchanged. Return on investment, not long-term protection of ecosystems, dominates as *the* decision criterion. Green technological trajectories can only emerge to produce greater ecological sustainability when there is a radical restructuring of the funding, organization, and direction of the innovation process (Gould 2006). Such restructuring requires the deep structural changes to the political economy prescribed by treadmill theory.[4]

Promoting greater efficiency in natural resource throughput as a means by which to sustain economic growth tends to ignore the structural nature of growth incentives and the constant imperative of expansion of even nominally Green firms (Schnaiberg and Gould 2000). These political and economic arrangements require constant expansion of productive capacity, so that efficiency gains (quality improvements) are bound to be offset eventually by output expansion (quantity increases). Reducing the levels of ecological withdrawals and additions per unit of production attains environmental gains only when levels of total output are kept steady. If total unit output is increased, as the logic of capital demands, greater efficiency of natural resource use offers only the potential for *more material consumption per level of ecological disorganization* (Schnaiberg and Gould 2000, 53–54). In effect, efficiency will shift the trade-off between material benefits and ecological disorganization in favor of material benefits. More material gains are achieved through the same levels of ecological disruption. In that sense, efficiency is likely to yield *greater* support for treadmill expansion.

Cooperative agreements with treadmill firms were championed by state, industry, and environmental organization elites under Third Wave environmentalism (Athanasiou 1996; Dowie 1995). Again, this approach fails to address the structure of capitalist political economies and the incentives and disincentives that structure offers private capital interests. Underlying Third Wave environmentalism is the naive assumption that negative environmental outcomes are a result of a lack of understanding of, or concern for, the ecological consequences of production. Here the mantra is "education is the key." We disagree. Rather, these ecological consequences are a result of the constraints and incentives structured into the economic terrain of most firms (Schnaiberg and Gould 2000). Regardless of managerial or investor levels of concern or understanding of ecological consequences, the competitive pressures of capitalism offer only antiecological trajectories for the survival of firms (Korten 2001).

Firms making proenvironmental choices, left to compete with firms making antiecological choices, are likely to fail in competitive systems. Antiecological choices are, after all, based precisely on the competitive *advantages* that these choices offer. Only changes to the array of incentives and disincentives can reduce the degree of competitive benefits bestowed on those firms that make antiecological choices. Such changes can result only from sociopolitical alteration of the larger macrostructural environment in which capital operates. State and broader public intervention in markets is a necessity for such change to occur, and yet that is precisely the action that cooperative agreements are intended to circumvent. Cooperative agreements also tend to focus on Green technologies and greater efficiencies, neither of which offers much potential for ecological sustainability within the rules of the current political economy of the treadmill.

It is understandable that, in an era where neoliberal markets dominate, environmentalists would increasingly attempt to find means by which the environment can be protected *within* a market-driven system. All other options promise a future full of difficult political conflicts with powerful actors and institutions, in which success appears highly unlikely. The structure of markets itself, though, represents the primary threat to ecological sustainability. Hence, efforts to resolve "free" market systems and ecosystems are less likely to succeed. For the serious analyst or activist, the *difficulty* presented by the treadmill model's prescription of confronting political-economic arrangements is offset by the *impossibility* of achieving environmental protection within those arrangements. Because of the extent that markets (private capital) have increasingly gained the ideological and political edge over policy (states) in the last 28 years, the possibilities for achieving ecological sustainability have grown dimmer. These observations are supported directly by statements made by free trade ministers and documented in free trade agreements, including NAFTA and GATT.

Similarly, voluntary simplicity efforts represent a retreat from environmental politics, which is the last thing we need at this historical moment. First, treadmill supporters and beneficiaries control the information environment in which individuals develop their needs, desires, choices, and views (Schiller 1996). Thus, it is unlikely that those eschewing material consumption are going to win the ideological battle for the hearts and minds of a global population, plugged into an advertising-driven information system (now expanded into the electronic domain of the Internet). Voluntary simplicity in the north is thus unlikely to achieve more than minor "cult" status out of a wide range of lifestyle choices. Since production leads consumption, only an overwhelming *mass* adoption of voluntary simplicity on a planetary scale offers much hope of altering the array of which material goods are *produced,* much less the *way* in which they are produced. Based on the notion of individual action rather than organization by mass movements, voluntary simplicity fails to offer the ideological and tactical orientation necessary to make it even marginally viable.

Green consumerism, voluntary simplicity's meek and mild cousin, offers even less potential. The location of production decisions is with capital producers. Their logic concerning growth and distribution emphasizes making only enough Green products to saturate existing markets. Most citizens cannot afford to abandon buying cheaper, non-Green products to meet their basic needs, because of the distributional logic of treadmill capital organizations. As noted earlier, cheaper goods produced for low wages and with high ecological costs in the global south are the primary means by which northern workers who face declining or stagnating wages have retained their standard of living. Adoption of individual consumer choice as a route toward sustainability is perhaps the most disheartening development, even more disheartening than the mainstream environmental movement's resistance to political conflict. The replacement of *collective* action and democratic governance with *individual* consumer choice represents a clear ideological victory for treadmill supporters. The neoliberal economists' desire to replace voting with shopping as the mechanism through which social interests are expressed threatens to eliminate the possibility of both democratic governance and environmental sustainability.

Of all of the currently popular means to achieve environmental ends, policy tinkering actually offers the greatest potential for achieving *some* increased levels of environmental protection as a route toward a more managed scarcity synthesis. Precisely because of the greater potential of policy intervention for constraining negative ecological impacts imposed by the logic of markets, it is now on the wane. Policy intervention in the operation of markets is precisely the democratic constraint on capital that neoliberalism intends to disable. Private capital interests have encouraged Third Wave environmentalism instead. While mild policy interventions do nothing to alter the basic growth and distributional logics of capital producers, they do offer the potential to adjust the constraints and incentives within which competitive capital may operate. Such policy interventions can increase the costs of antiecological choices for all firms, thus decreasing the competitive disadvantages associated with proenvironmental choices.

Policy intervention can also generate incentives for *some* alteration of technological trajectories and may preclude *some* forms of production. As capital becomes increasingly transnational in its scope of operation, however, policy intervention remains largely a phenomenon on a national level. Paradoxically, though, national policy intervention is likely to increase incentives for firms to locate production primarily in low-regulatory environments (Schnaiberg and Gould 2000). Yet, given the social consequences of disincentives for *domestic* production, states are increasingly reticent to intervene in markets to protect the environment.

In a global economy, only global policy interventions can alter the competitive environment in which firms make fewer or more ecologically protective decisions. Yet, no viable institutional structures currently exist for the imposition and enforcement of such global policy interventions. This realization is an important motivating factor behind the emergence of a transnational anti–corporate globalization movement.

Power, Inequality, and Redistribution

Most of the generally accepted mechanisms for achieving greater levels of environmental protection that have already been mentioned ignore the central role of social inequality in generating support for antiecological economic trajectories. So, too, do most mainstream environmental organizations. Treadmill support is generated, in part, by the promise of alleviating the poverty-related impacts of capitalism through economic expansion rather than through social redistribution. Without a redistributive option, the current political economy offers either perpetual, deepening impoverishment of a growing segment of the population or a trickling down of limited economic benefits through accelerating antiecological growth.

What makes the treadmill model so threatening to state, capital, and movement elites is that it strongly advocates a move toward a steady state economy. There, most forms of economic *growth* are precluded to achieve ecologically sustainable *development*.[5] Under such conditions, the only route toward poverty alleviation domestically and transnationally is *redistribution* resulting from state intervention in or dismantlement of market systems. Redistribution thus becomes an essential component of any effort to achieve sustainability. Without the promise of redistribution, citizen-workers are unlikely to accept the low- or no-growth trajectories needed to protect ecosystems, except under conditions of extreme levels of repression (Stretton 1976). Repression is costly, however, both economically and ecologically. Ultimately, it may prove socially and ecologically unsustainable (Gould 2007). For all these reasons, then, redistribution is the key to achieving sustainable development and securing broad support for slowing or dismantling the treadmill.

The combined critique of the antiecological logic of capital and the necessity of more equitable distribution within a no- or slow-growth economy makes the treadmill model threatening to capital elites, in particular, and their clients (state elites). The model is also threatening to the economically privileged groups that most commonly comprise the leadership and core funding membership of mainstream environmental organizations. Steady state economies with equitable distribution as the model for social and ecological sustainability also threaten the many Green Party organizations that naively champion slogans such as "neither left nor right, but forward."

The treadmill model denies the possibility of making an ecological end run around distributional (class) politics, even as it problematizes the structural role of workers within the political economy (Gould 2006). Transnationalization of the economy and deepening global inequality make the possibility of avoiding distributional politics in pursuit of Green objectives decreasingly plausible. Inequality provides the basis for environmental injustices, insatiable material aspirations, antiecological survival strategies, and treadmill support even in the face of ever-diminishing social returns. The treadmill model powerfully argues that any attempted solution to environmental problems that does not adequately address the distributional dimensions of socioenvironmental dynamics is unworkable. In doing so, the model indicates that political conflict with the ruling elite is inevitable and must be waged successfully to achieve socioenvironmental sustainability. This brings the entire repressive apparatus of states dependent on economic elites to bear on treadmill opponents and redistribution advocates.

In addition to the treadmill model's implications for capital actors, the theory of the state within the model also implies certain political opportunities and constraints. By focusing on treadmill elites and their interests, the model does indicate a greater orientation toward conceptualization of the role, and nature, of the state in terms of dependence on capital elites (Domhoff 1998; Gonzalez 2001). The model does allow for the emergence of greater state autonomy in specific historical periods and under certain socioeconomic and political conditions. The drift of states *away from* redistributive policies and market intervention, however, since *The Environment* was first published in 1980 is an indication of a greater capture of the state by economic elites. This has led us in later iterations of our work to emphasize elite convergence, rather than a state-autonomy conceptualization (Skocpol 1980). Even under specific historical conditions that might produce capital-state elite schisms (paralleling the Great Depression), labor and consumer support of the treadmill is likely to produce a more pluralist politics that would still support growth. This is so unless the extent of the environmental crises was accepted generally *and* strong redistributive policies were put in place. A more autonomous state pursuing its own independently structured interests would be more open to citizen-worker appeals for environmental and public health protections. Although this mechanism of treadmill deceleration is open to more political control, it does not necessarily indicate that structural solutions would *automatically* be advocated.

Ecological consciousness-raising, therefore, has some power to decelerate the treadmill through policy tinkering. This power is diminished, however, as firms operate on transnational rather than national structural terrains. With the threat of dramatic negative economic consequences, globalization has affected the willingness and the ability of states to effectively intervene in markets. Therefore, ecological consciousness-raising must emerge in more transnational organizations rather than primarily through participation in domestic political processes (although the structure of the transnational environmental movement remains problematic; see Lewis 2000, 2003). Within the transnational economic system, some southern states are even less capable than the United States or other northern states of advancing the proenvironmental claims of a collectively organized citizenry. Yet transnational mobilization is perhaps the only viable path toward social and ecological sustainability. That such efforts will succeed in the face of the powerful forces aligned against them is problematic at best.

Police defend a bank after protesters break through a barricade protecting thirty-four heads of state negotiating the proposed Free Trade Area of the Americas in Quebec City, 2001. (photo by Ken Gould)

CHAPTER 8

Conclusion

The Clarifying Lines of Conflict

Production Trends Accelerating the Treadmill of Production

The Reign of the Private over the Public Sector

IT IS NOW MORE THAN A QUARTER CENTURY since the introduction of the treadmill theory. These 28 years have seen some major economic and political changes. We have scientifically traced some of these in our prior work and in this book. Here we attempt to provide an analytic and action *framework* for scholars and activists, to consider the goals and means of social movements to offer progressive change to the globalizing treadmill. This chapter illustrates these changes with some empirical examples.

Some changes have centered on issues of the role of the public versus the private sector. Others are associated with a variety of expansions of international trade and the rise of "globalization." As noted later, these have the potential to dramatically change relations between the north and the south—for better or for worse.

What links these two dimensions of change from 1980–2008 is a sharply declining role of government agencies in the United States (and in other countries to lesser degrees) in maintaining, creating, and expanding new forms of social welfare. A landmark shift within the United States has been the "welfare-to-work" programs introduced by the Clinton-Gore administration, which have moved social welfare payments off the government rolls.

These programs have coerced recipients to seek private-sector work by placing a time limit on their receipt of public welfare benefits. We stress *private*-sector employment as recipients' major alternative, in part because this same "liberal" U.S. administration simultaneously downsized the federal government workforce by about 25 percent.

The subsequent U.S. presidential administration of George W. Bush further constrained governments by creating substantial tax cuts, largely designed to support the wealthiest class (the top 2 percent of income earners) and large corporations. This move not only reduced the federal government's capacity to expand employment but also limited state and local governments' capacity to do so. Each level of state administration has been forced to downsize its workforce. Thus, displaced welfare recipients' only option for employment has been in the private sector, which, unfortunately, has not been a reliable source of job creation over the last quarter century either.

If this were the only set of changes, it would strongly signal a shift in the United States from "politics" to "markets" (Lindblom 1977). Under changing conditions in the distribution of employment, the state was induced to expand its support for business growth. Politicians needed to rein in potential political opposition from working- and middle-class constituents. As individuals, the working and middle classes lack political power, unlike that of treadmill corporations (Weinberg and Schnaiberg 2001). But they also have had powerful allies—union political action programs, progressive politicians, and some social movements. Given a choice, however, between expanding the government's budget (derived from increased taxes) or increasing the profits of the private sector (derived from the expansion of production), the U.S. government chose to support the expansion of the private sector. This fit the conservative agenda of "small government," directly reducing corporate taxes and indirectly lowering corporate operating costs by paring back regulatory activity, especially the enforcement of environmental protection and labor laws.

Paradoxically, while the state was reducing its employment levels, the private sector was downsizing much of its own workforce. Under the rubric of "increased global competitiveness" and support from the growing electronic and chemical technology industries, many middle-class and working-class jobs were terminated. In addition, jobs were "outsourced" because of U.S. investments and production abroad. Interestingly, although there has been recent political mobilization against this latter trend (including during the 2004 and 2008 presidential campaigns), it appears that far more jobs have been lost because of technological introductions within the United States (Reich 1991). For example, several years ago it was estimated that if all U.S. auto plants introduced robotics (the technology used in Toyota's U.S. operations), more than 125,000 United Automobile Workers (UAW) union jobs would be lost nationwide. Such issues concerning the control and direction of technological innovation have largely been organized out of domestic political discourse (Gould 2006).

Whatever the reality of technological "advancements" versus outsourcing as the causes of declining employment, the overall effect has been to produce more pressure on the state to offer incentives to corporations to expand in general and to increase their exports in particular. Conversely, the state's reduction of taxes on wealthy taxpayers has expanded their potential to divert even more of their wealth to overseas investments, where they can anticipate a higher rate of return. Both corporate and personal tax decisions undermine the trickle-down theories of "supply-side economics" (Krugman 2002, 2003), which led to the huge deficits during the Reagan administration in the 1980s. The basic argument has been that reducing taxes on wealthy investors leads them to invest in new commercial activities, which in turn generate more jobs. Yet this flies in the face of the history of the modern treadmill. Supply-side economic arguments and policies have been rejuvenated regarding the Bush administration's deficits during 2001–2008, with the same illusory distributive outcomes. The gaps between the poor and the wealthy have, predictably, increased, and spending on social and environmental programs has been cut, while resources have been diverted to support investors and military projects. In that sense, the size of government is less an issue than its shifting emphasis toward support for privatization, militarization, and the prison-industrial complex.

From this labor-absorption process alone, we can see why environmental protection activities of the state have been constrained.

The state has a shrinking share of the GNP and has faced an exponential increase in political demands to "create jobs" by growing the private sector. To the more traditional political pressure by working-class constituents have been added articulate demands by more politically powerful middle-class constituents whose *own* job prospects have been reduced (Derber 1998; Ehrenreich 1990; Leicht and Fitzgerald 2007). Thus, both the state's *capacity* to protect ecosystems, and its *political will* have shrunk. Even during the business expansion of the mid-1990s, there were only small increases in the EPA's efforts, most of them embracing neoconservative paradigms like "flexible regulation" and voluntary initiatives (under the Clinton-Gore administration), which laid the groundwork for the more intensive laissez-faire policies of the George W. Bush regime.

As noted earlier, it is also the case that the United States has focused on reducing toxic hazards more than on reducing the corporate extraction/production that destroys large components of natural habitats. Perhaps the best symbolic representation of this dynamic has been the recurring debate on oil drilling in the Arctic National Wildlife Refuge (ANWR). While the measure has not yet passed, it has been proposed repeatedly in the last decade in Congress—and in the case of the Bush administration, with strong political support from the White House. Numerous related developments give us pause when we consider the future of environmental politics in this nation. Several examples follow.

In fiscal year 2003, the White House allowed the federal Superfund toxic waste cleanup program to run out of polluter-contributed funds, leaving taxpayers to pay the projected annual rate of $1.1 billion for the program. Congressman John Dingell stated, "The Bush administration has dramatically decreased cleanups and opposed efforts to renew the polluter taxes." The Sierra Club's Executive Director Carl Pope declared, "It's unconscionable for the Bush administration not to hold polluters responsible for the cleanup of toxic waste. Polluters, not taxpayers, should be footing the bill" (ENS 2004d). The "polluter pays" principle was the key underpinning of the Superfund concept.

Another example is the national Energy Task Force, chaired by Vice President Dick Cheney in 2001. Not only was the task force composed primarily of representatives of major U.S. energy conglomerates (including Enron Corporation), its meetings took place within congressional chambers. This was truly a case of the fox in the chicken coop, reassuring the public that "all is well" (Weinberg et al. 1996). Among other outcomes of this committee was a strong statement supporting oil drilling in ANWR—not surprising since there were no environmental protection advocates on the committee. In May 2001, when elected officials, environmentalists, and public interest advocates demanded disclosure of the substance of those meetings and the names of participating industries on the committee, the Bush regime refused to provide access to any information—one of many acts of state secrecy that has raised serious questions about the state of democracy in the United States.

Critics' concerns were justified when, one week later, the Bush regime announced its National Energy Policy, which heavily favored fossil fuels and nuclear power over renewable energy, energy efficiency, and energy conservation (Pegg 2004). A similar struggle occurred regarding the EPA's granting special access to a task force of agrochemical corporations that advocated that the agency circumvent the Endangered Species Act by allowing pesticide uses that harm federally protected species (ENS 2004c). In direct violation of the Federal Advisory Committee Act, the EPA met in secret with representatives of 14 pesticide-producing corporations (including Monsanto, Dow, BASF, and FMC) with no input from the public or environmentalists. The Federal Insecticide, Fungicide, and Rodenticide Act (FIFRA) was amended by the Endangered Species Task Force, which pressed for the weakening of pesticide safeguards by eliminating expert oversight in the implementation of federal regulations.

The Bush White House is also infamous for its abandonment and repudiation of the 1997 Kyoto Protocol, the international agreement among nations to reduce greenhouse gases linked to climate change. The defiance of Kyoto was the pinnacle of a broader corporate and political campaign to undermine the scientific record on global warming research. Included in this resistance was the Competitive Enterprise Institute's (CEI) efforts to (1) rewrite or remove research reports by government scientists that revealed the serious nature of global warming; and (2) "get rid of" EPA officials who supported global warming research, including EPA chief Christine Whitman (Harris 2003). CEI received more than $1 million in donations from the Exxon Corporation alone between

1998 and 2003, so the objectives of the institute's activities were clear. CEI has close ties with the Bush regime, and its influence in the White House has been considerable.

No less scandalous was the administration's attempt (later withdrawn) to weaken a Clinton-era proposal to reduce the permissible level of arsenic in drinking water (Barringer 2004). Regarding both arsenic and global warming, George W. Bush argued that there "was no scientific consensus" on these matters. So in classic "risk-assessment" form (in contrast to the precautionary principle),[1] the construction of scientific "uncertainty" allowed treadmill elites to err on the side of allowing polluting corporations to continue with business as usual. Conservative think tanks expend great effort to generate such scientific uncertainty from outside the academic peer-review system (Beder 1997). In June 2004, 4000 scientists—including 42 Nobel laureates—protested publicly that the White House had been distorting science for political purposes (Buncombe 2004). The Bush administration's solution to environmental protection appears to be a mixture of free-market principles and "volunteerism," both of which are aimed at encouraging environmental stewardship through gutting regulations and assuming corporate responsibility rather than through legal or structural protections (ENS 2004a).

These conflicts strongly suggest a turn from a managed scarcity synthesis of the societal-environmental dialectic toward a more traditional economic synthesis—which largely dismisses ecological concerns (Schnaiberg 1980). Although ecological modernization theorists proclaim the proliferation of new production technologies that might be compatible with sustainable development, it is difficult to see much of this evident in the U.S. political-economic processes of the last quarter century.

The Penetration of Social Institutions by a Treadmill Culture

This is not the full extent of the surge of the treadmill influence, however, into what Lindblom (1977) might have called the "subversion of politics by the market." With the decline in revenues and in public oversight of governments, new opportunities have been opened for novel forms of treadmill influence. Strained municipal budgets, for example, have permitted corporations to supply equipment (such as vehicles) to local governments, complete with corporate logos. In some way, this provides a new form of "branding" of the state by corporate images. While there has been much public and litigious controversy about the independence of "church and state," far less attention has been paid to the unabated integration of "market and state." In part, this is due to the formal restraint in the U.S. Constitution on church/state relationships. The degree to which the market has penetrated all forms of governmental decision making, however, has been far subtler and more pervasive (Lowi 1979; Korten 2001).

Moreover, this new penetration goes well beyond earlier concerns about the "capture" of state regulatory agencies by the industries they were supposed to regulate (e.g., Weinberg et al. 1996). The latter involved a circulation of elites between state agencies and regulated industries. More recently, though, the private sector has had unparalleled influence on public policy making, to the extent that the boundaries between "public" as distinct from "private" are often blurred or eliminated.

Nor are state regulatory agencies the only sites of new treadmill penetration. Universities and colleges increasingly have become directly influenced by corporate funding. In previous decades, a substantial share of university funding came from government agencies. The state collected corporate taxes and allocated some of them to environmental "impact research" (Schnaiberg 1975) by university faculty and researchers. Corporations only had indirect control of some of this process, through participation in hearings on the budgets of federal scientific agencies. In contrast, "production research" was also carried out by both universities and corporate research and development departments. In these cases, corporate grants to research teams supported such production research—helping to generate new products and new processes (Noble 1977). With the decline in federal scientific budgets, though, direct corporate influence on university agendas has broadened (White 2000).

Perhaps the most striking case was that of the Microbiology Department of the University of California at Berkeley. The department as a whole accepted a $25-million grant from the Novartis Corporation (now Syngenta), for a five-year period. In public, there was a disclaimer by both sides that the corporation exerted no "undue influence" on the university. Moreover, an independent committee, headed by a sociological researcher, Lawrence Busch of Michigan State University, affirmed this judgment. However, in private correspondence, Busch indicated grave concerns about the autonomy of researchers posed by this novel arrangement. The cautions are twofold: (1) university researchers are well rewarded for doing production research that Novartis might develop into new, profitable products/processes; and/or (2) researchers conducting impact assessments on the products of Novartis or the broader pharmaceutical and agrochemical industries might avoid carrying out research and disseminating it to a scientific and lay public, for fear of jeopardizing future grants.

In addition to these structural penetrations by treadmill organizations are a variety of "cultural" penetrations. Both sporting facilities and many school programs have been embedded with corporate logos and name branding, further identifying the treadmill firms with the community's functions (White 2000). There certainly have been precedents, such as the provision of automobiles for public high school drivers' education programs (incidentally, building a future consumer base). But there is really little precedent for the increased blending of the private-sector with public/collective functions.

At one university in the Rocky Mountain region, football players were told that they must wear the Nike Corporation's logo (the "swoosh") on their person at all times during team practices and games. Players who came to practices without clothing bearing the logo were subject to dismissal. This mandate was a core part of the university's contract with that corporation. Many players wanted to protest this requirement, particularly given their awareness of Nike's contracts with sweatshop operators in Southeast Asia. But their dissent was silenced by the prospect of their termination. At that same university in 2000, the dean of the College of Arts and Sciences met with every department in the college to promote the idea of seeking corporate grants for research and for general institutional support. One professor asked the dean, "Does this mean that one day we might have a 'Coca Cola Department of Sociology'?" The dean replied, "Absolutely! That's exactly the kind of vision I'm talking about." A few years later, a prominent instructor well known for having her students research the criminal behavior of corporations who did business with the university was unceremoniously fired. Areas of university life that were previously off limits to corporate influence, or at least not subject to such an intense level of control and sanction by corporations, are now totally vulnerable (White 2000). Under these conditions the very purpose of higher education is in question and at risk.

How Militarization Expands the Treadmill and Reduces Resistance to It

An often-overlooked dimension of the treadmill of production is the impact of the military (and the broader problem of militarism) on the environment and society (Hooks and Smith 2004). Specifically, the U.S. military is one of the largest sources of pollution in the nation and is a major polluter globally. While far too many U.S. academics have been silent on this issue, some scholars have been quite openly critical of the U.S. military-industrial complex, referring to it as a core component of this nation's empire-building activities (Chomsky 1993; Hardt and Negri 2001; Johnson 2000). Given that the United States has more than 700 military bases around the world and the largest nuclear and military arsenals of any nation, this characterization seems appropriate. Despite (or because of) the intense levels of pollution generated by the U.S. military, the Department of Defense (DoD) has repeatedly urged that it be exempted from a host of federal environmental regulations; and the White House has supported this push, in the name of "national security."

Building on previous exemptions from the Marine Mammal Protection Act and the Endangered Species Act, the DoD and the White House asked Congress for exemptions from provisions of the Clean Air Act and the two major federal toxic waste cleanup laws—the Resource Conservation and Recovery Act (RCRA) and the Comprehensive Environmental Response, Compensation, and Liability Act (CERCLA) (Luoma 2003). In May 2004, General Anders Aadland, head of the Army's Installation Management Command, ordered military bases across the nation to halt anti-pollution and wildlife protection spending because of fiscal shortages associated with "fighting a war on several fronts" (ENS

2004b). Thus, with government approval, the military has succeeded in achieving special treatment with regard to environmental regulations. As the U.S. military becomes more privatized, its overall accountability shifts further away from public scrutiny and control (Goodman 2003).

While the military itself has produced its own treadmill of violence and ecological devastation, the broader, deeper concern is the spread of *militarism* domestically and globally. Militarism is "a vast array of customs, interests, prestige, actions, and thought associated with armies and wars and yet transcending true military purpose" (Vagts 1937: 11). That is, when the military mindset and culture are institutionalized in society, the transformation creates a public mobilized by fear and despair (thus, often resulting in *im*mobility) rather than the desire for sustainability, social justice, and cooperation.

The "War on Terror" then plays nicely into the hands of corporations that might otherwise be concerned with the impact of social protest on their activities and on shareholder value. Activists who campaign against various unsavory practices associated with natural resource extraction, pollution, wage depression, loss of benefits (e.g., health care and pensions), and increased workdays/workweeks are treated as potential security threats. And while corporate power may often trump state power, we should not make the mistake of believing that the state has "withered away." Rather, as the progressive Russian economist Boris Kagarlitsky argues, globalization does not produce state impotence; instead, it is generally accompanied by "the rejection by the state of its social function, in favor of repressive ones, and the ending of democratic freedoms" (Kagarlitsky 2001).

Will the Treadmill Collapse or Be Dismantled?

There is no question that the trend in both domestic and transnational political economies over the past 28 years has been toward deepening the commitment to treadmill values and treadmill acceleration. The (re-)election of George W. Bush in 2004 is one component of this trend. So are the spread and entrenchment of neoliberal economic theory throughout the global south and the former Eastern bloc. These diffused ideologies and practices portend even more intransigent national and supranational institutional support for the expansion of the treadmill of production. The results of treadmill acceleration and expansion have not been surprising. Across almost every dimension, the deterioration of the natural environment has quickened. Global waste streams have grown larger and more pernicious, habitat destruction has accelerated, and both renewable and nonrenewable natural resource consumption has increased steadily. The socioenvironmental and public health costs of growing ecological degradation have been systematically distributed downward through the transnational socioeconomic strata, as the treadmill has generated ever-increasing economic inequality within and between countries. Such heightening class polarization has simultaneously allowed the small minority of global-elite beneficiaries of treadmill growth to isolate and insulate themselves from much of the social and ecological consequences of their production decisions and policies (Gould 2006).

Without the emergence of some powerful countervailing social force, the future is likely to offer deepening global inequality, widespread poverty, and irrecoverable destruction of the ecosystem. The insular world of the treadmill elite grows ever-more removed from the lived experience of most of the planet's inhabitants. Clearly, then, the planetary history of the past 28 years has been good for neither the maintenance of ecological integrity nor the realization of a socially equitable development trajectory.

The treadmill of production, however, is neither immutable nor inevitable. Recent history demonstrates a strong trend toward treadmill entrenchment. Yet those societies that have adopted treadmill ideology and structures can adopt *alternative* development trajectories that may be more congruent with social justice, ecological and human health, and long-term sustainability. Perhaps more inevitable than the triumph of the global treadmill is its ultimate collapse or dismantlement. If the treadmill *is* truly unsustainable both socially and ecologically, at some point it must either exhaust the planet's capacity to provide economically necessary resource pools and waste sinks or produce such deep, widespread social suffering that the vast majority forcibly dismantles it.

As social scientists, it is beyond the scope of our expertise to assess the natural science reports of global ecological collapse. Recent reports on the state of the ecosystem appear, however, to be converging. Professionals with expertise in assessing environmental conditions now widely believe that the world's oceans are in or near a state of ecological collapse. The global climate is experiencing a rapid and dramatic shift at least partly induced by human activity. Forests, wetlands, mangroves, coral reefs, and other especially rich ecological features are rapidly dwindling. The biological diversity of the planet is decreasing at a rate that defines evolutionary epochs. Freshwater aquifers are being drained well beyond recharge rates.

Thus far, this mounting ecological disorganization has done little to slow the treadmill. Paradoxically, each dimension of ecological collapse offers new opportunities for treadmill expansion. Global warming generates markets for air conditioners. Diminishing freshwater supplies create World Bank support of markets for privatized water (Goldman 2005). Drought and desertification produces demand for genetically modified, privatized agricultural organisms (Buttel 1997). Dwindling petroleum sources spurs investment by the major auto manufacturers in electric and hybrid power automobiles. Habitat destruction raises the premium for access to protected ecotourism resorts. Likewise, seafood scarcity creates opportunities for aquaculture investment. The treadmill of production is thus able to capitalize on the very ecological destruction that it generates. This is a good indicator that the ecological limit to treadmill expansion may be relatively distant. It is certainly an indicator that waiting for ecological limits to ultimately force the treadmill to slow or be dismantled will result in a natural world that is highly degraded and virtually unrecognizable to that of 28 years ago or even today (Redclift 1987). This is also evidence of the triumph of "markets over politics" (Lindblom 1977), which reveals a deepening global culture of faith in the marketplace and in new technologies for solutions to social problems.

If counting on the exhaustion of global resource pools and waste sinks to render the treadmill untenable is far too costly ecologically (and therefore socially), we must look to the emergence of countervailing social forces to prohibit the treadmill's socioeconomic acceleration over the ecological precipice. As social scientists, we are in a position to describe, analyze, and assess the social developments that indicate a growing intolerance for the social and ecological impacts of the treadmill's trajectory. Despite the overall trend toward greater institutional commitment to the treadmill, we see the potential for a convergence of new and old social forces in response to this deepening crisis. These forces may develop the capacity to substantially slow, alter, or replace the treadmill. The reaction of a growing segment of the global population to the socioecological costs of a globalized treadmill of production is decidedly negative. While structural coercion forces most states, institutions, communities, and individuals to act in some way to support treadmill expansion, resistance is evident and growing. Moreover, some theories of revolution note that revolutionary actions occur not at the point of deepest despair, but just when some resistance has been mobilized already (Gurr 1971). If this is so, then recent social and political reactions to the treadmill may be early indicators that both ecological and social limits are approaching.

Antitreadmill Trends: Resistance and Social Movements

Because the treadmill of production is a global phenomenon, challenges to this system must also operate globally, while building strength at the local level. Transnational social movement organizations (TSMOs) are proliferating and have been since the dawn of the post–World War II era. "Between 1953 and 1993, the population of TSMOs grew from less than 200 to more than 600 organizations" (Smith et al. 1997). Parallel to this rise in transnational political activism was the proliferation of global communication technologies. These changes expanded the capacity of government, businesses, and social movements to organize across national boundaries on much larger scales than they had in even the early part of the twentieth century (ibid.: 96). TSMOs are now widely acknowledged as formidable players in international politics because they are creating new global norms and practices among states, international bodies, and corporations, and transforming old ones (e.g., see Keck and Sikkink 1998; Lewis 2000).

Such "non-state actors" can be viewed as sources of resistance to globalization "from below" (Khagram et al. 2002: 4).

Global environmental justice, labor, and human rights networks are challenging states and corporations to meet acceptable codes of conduct and to comply with international law. The Stockholm Convention on Persistent Organic Pollutants, the Basel Convention (on the global waste trade), the Montreal Protocol (on the reduction of chlorofluorocarbons [CFCs]), and a range of other international environmental agreements were negotiated in part by TSMOs and NGOs. But since these are multiple stakeholder groups controlled primarily by states and TNCs, peoples' movements have limited efficacy and thus still need autonomous political spaces from which to produce new models for social change.

For example, the World Social Forum (WSF) and its spin-offs in Europe, the United States, and throughout the global south have evolved as the people's alternative to the World Economic Forum's annual meeting among heads of state and Fortune 500 companies. Since 2001, the WSF has met in Brazil, India, Venezuela, Mali, Pakistan, and Kenya to discuss and strategize about campaigns against privatization, environmental destruction, and militarization throughout the global south. A major global campaign to boycott World Bank bonds gained strength at the WSF. Ties between NGOs in the north and south have also improved as a result of WSF gatherings where the rallying cry is "Another World Is Possible." This cry is a powerful, discursive framing of history and the future. It challenges the global, neoliberal ideological view that might be summed up as "this world is the best of all possible worlds, and the current situation is inevitable." The struggle against the "psychology of inevitability" (Gedicks 1993) is perhaps the first major hurdle in building a resistance movement against the global treadmill.

Scholars and activists have noted for some time that a recurring concern among activists and residents in the global south is that TSMOs (and, by extension, transnational civil society itself) overwhelmingly represent the concerns of northerners (Gould 2003; Lewis 2003). The latter are endowed with greater resources and often have distinct interests and histories (Florini 2000: 6). This tension mirrors the conflicts scholars have observed between white middle-class environmentalists and environmental justice activists from working-class backgrounds and communities of color in the United States (Roberts and Toffolon-Weiss 2000). For north-south alliances to be successful in the long term, they have to be more than just "fragile fax-and-cyberspace skeletons" that lack any long-term direction (Fox and Brown 1998); they must develop respect and trust, and most importantly, they must be able to summon and command material and structural power. This success will not come easily. A positive sign is the development of many transnational NGOs in the north who recognize the need for developing global solutions to environmental problems. Many of these groups are beginning to acknowledge that the north is creating much of the ecological damage confronting the south. Greenpeace, Global Response, Friends of the Earth, and the Global Alliance for Incinerator Alternatives are all organizing around these political approaches.

Many scholars question whether international NGOs have actually had any enduring impact on the structural conditions giving rise to environmental degradation and poverty around the world. Sklair (2002), for example, argues that TSMOs have failed fundamentally to challenge and restructure global capital. He also argues that (following Piven and Cloward 1979), to be successful, TSMOs will have to disrupt capitalism first at the local level and then find ways of globalizing these disruptions. His central claim is that, although capital is increasingly global in this era, effective opposition to its excesses occurs largely through local manifestations. Sklair takes seriously the question of political economy and the role of corporations as targets by movements. He is also clear that, to have an impact, movements must have the power to challenge "business as usual":

> Where the TNCs have been disrupted to the extent that their hegemony has been weakened and even where, in some cases, they have been forced to change their ways and compensate those who have grievances against them, it has usually been due to local campaigns of direct action and counter information against TNC malpractices that have attracted worldwide publicity. There are sufficient cases (the Distillers' Company thalidomide tragedy, Union Carbide's Bhopal disaster, various oil companies' environmental catastrophes, ongoing campaigns against Nestlé's infant formula, logging companies, etc.) to suggest that such single-issue

social movements do have genuine disruptive effects in curbing the worst excesses of profiteering TNCs. (Sklair 2002: 299)

Sklair maintains that when activists can constantly disrupt, monitor, and shame TNCs into behaving responsibly, this amounts to a challenge to capitalist hegemony.

While northern movements gain ground, the leadership of the global environmental justice struggle will have to come primarily from the south. Roy (2004) argues that, in general, there are two kinds of mass resistance movements in the south today. One is typified by "the landless peoples' movement in Brazil, the anti-dam movement in India, the Zapatistas in Mexico, the Anti-Privatization Forum in South Africa, and hundreds of others that are fighting their own sovereign governments, which have become agents of the neo-liberal project." Roy views most of these movements as "radical" because they are struggling to challenge the nature of "development" in their societies.

The other kind of resistance movement today consists of revolts against "brutal neocolonial occupations in contested territories whose boundaries and fault lines were often arbitrarily drawn last century by the imperialist powers" (ibid.). Examples include Palestine, Tibet, Chechnya, and Kashmir, where people are fighting for self-determination. The first kind of struggle is often more progressive than the second. As a result of the brutality of the repression the latter faces, political movements are frequently pushed into reactionary and conservative spaces "in which they use the same violent strategies and the same language of religious and cultural nationalism used by the states they seek to replace" (Roy 2004). This will continue to be a challenge for peoples' movements, as the level of brutality and repression they face escalates in a world where the treadmill of production and militarism are intensifying.

A Convergence of Treadmill Resistance and Crises?

Despite the apparent insurgency of protreadmill forces in the past 28 years, we see signs of a convergence of the kinds of resistance just noted in the following economic, political, and cultural developments:

- the erosion of the Washington Consensus and direct challenges to U.S. hegemony, especially among the states of Latin America;
- the emergence of an increasingly unified, transnational anti-corporate globalization movement;
- the global proliferation of local and regional autonomist development alternatives;
- the transnationalization of the labor movement;
- the decreasing legitimacy of supranational treadmill institutions such as the IMF, World Bank, and WTO;
- the growing grassroots demand for meaningful radical democratization of policy making.

None of these developments *alone* is likely to prove an insurmountable obstacle to the treadmill. But the *convergence* of these social forces may indicate that widespread support for an alternative development trajectory is beginning to take shape—precisely the kinds of structures needed to actually determine if "another world is possible" (Hawken 2007).

The so-called Washington Consensus among global economic elites is that neoliberal globalization benefits everyone and represents the only viable global development trajectory. This ideology has become increasingly discredited, and not just in the south. There is increasing divergence among political elites in the industrialized world about the costs and benefits of many elements of transnational trade liberalization, most notably between those of the United States and EU member countries (McMichael 2004). Disagreements have emerged from specific sectors of liberalization. For example, in agriculture, questions regarding the safety of genetically modified crops have opened up political space for a deeper questioning of the course and efficacy of the current model of global trade regimes (Buttel and Gould 2005). This northern industrial elite schism has developed over an ostensibly *environmental* issue like the proliferation of genetically modified organisms. The emergence of such a schism indicates that some ecological, as well as social, ramifications of the treadmill have weakened what in the recent past was a unified front emanating from treadmill state elites.

Similarly, the outcomes of recent elections (and popular revolts) in Latin America have brought to power political parties and political elites who at least rhetorically reject the Washington Consensus prescriptions for southern poverty and global inequality. The failure of neoliberal development schemes to reduce both poverty and inequality, which in fact have deepened both, has led recently democratized populations to place critics of this approach in power in Brazil, Ecuador, Venezuela, Bolivia, Uruguay, and elsewhere. Although these newly elected governments are still constrained by the current global political economy, a growing consensus among southern governments that the global development trajectory must be rethought and reconfigured has generated much wider debate at the highest policy-making levels. Furthermore, support from the U.S. Congress and White House for efforts to undermine many of these elected officials and their governments suggests that these developments in the global south are viewed as potentially significant challenges to neoliberalism.

The focus of this debate is, admittedly, much more on transnational inequality than on ecological concerns. Yet the increasing rejection in the global south of the privatization of common natural resources by TNCs has major implications. It opens up new directions for the national and transnational management of increasingly scarce ecosystem elements. It is also important to note that what northerners often define as "ecological" concerns (clean water, food security, etc.) are, in fact, at the center of the public agenda for most southerners, but these issues are generally framed in association with poverty and survival. This is the real force behind the global grassroots resistance to the privatization of nature. Similar developments in other regions of the south have combined to forestall, perhaps fatally, the millennial round of WTO negotiations. This indicates that the neoliberal project may have reached a crisis of legitimacy. The resulting conflicts have placed the future global development trajectory back on the political agenda. There, the outcomes of debate and negotiation increasingly are contested and problematic.

Such political resistance has been generated by social movements within nations empowered by their growing integration into the wider transnational network of anti-corporate globalization activism. This coalition of movements against specific aspects of the neoliberal project that has stemmed from broader analyses of the social and ecological impacts of the neoliberal regime has gained significant power in recent years. Initially, these coalitions emerged from the anti-IMF "riots" in the global south in the 1970s in response to structural adjustment policies that deepened poverty and widened inequality (Walton and Seddon 1994). Since then, the movement has expanded through accretion, as various movements throughout the world have come to reject the negative consequences of the global treadmill. The movement now includes:

- European farmers seeking to protect their rural communities, modes of production, and genetic agricultural heritage;
- landless peasants in Brazil seeking to sustain their livelihoods;
- U.S. environmentalists seeking to maintain their hard-won environmental protection legislation;
- northern industrial workers seeking to save their jobs;
- human rights advocates seeking to secure access to health care and education for the world's poor; and
- southern movement activists seeking to maintain and expand access to affordable and safe potable water supplies.

A myriad of other groups in this "movement of movements" are attempting to achieve social justice, ecological integrity, meaningful democracy, and truly sustainable development (Danaher 2001; Danaher and Burbach 2000; George et al. 2001; Mertes 2004). Through education and mobilization, this loose coalition has brought into global focus the historical policies of the Bretton Woods institutions, the WTO, and neoliberal globalization in general. The movement has thus far succeeded in:

- empowering southern governments to stymie northern elite plans for the millennial round of WTO negotiations;

- preventing a "strong" FTAA from being realized;
- achieving significant (although insufficient) debt relief from international lending institutions for the most indebted nations; and
- making a wider swath of the global population aware of the negative ecological and social impacts of globalization.

The ecological dimensions of the anti-corporate globalization movement are significant. Northern mainstream environmental organizations that initially supported or were ambiguous about trade liberalization are now quite firmly in the antineoliberalism camp. The northern wing of the movement (especially in the United States in the lead-up to the November 1999 WTO protests in Seattle) was largely activated by the antienvironmental rulings of the WTO and NAFTA (Buttel and Gould 2004). The southern wing of the movement has focused great attention on the ecological costs of structural adjustment policies that mandate rapid increases in natural resource exports, generating the acceleration of habitat destruction. The movement's general focus has been:

- constraining corporate power and government capture by private capital in the battle against privatization of natural resources;
- working against the dissemination of genetically modified crop monocultures and megadevelopment projects that devastate ecosystems; and
- advocating against the violation of indigenous people's traditional territories in the exploration for and extraction of unexploited natural resources.

These developments have produced a truly global grassroots environmental movement. Such a movement is able to both "monitor locally and mobilize extralocally" in defense of ecological integrity (Gould et al. 1996). As a global coalition including both labor and environmental activists, the anti-corporate globalization movement has emerged as the lead, and in fact the only, broad social movement that is a strong countervailing force against the treadmill of production, organizing at the levels at which capital operates.

Various local, national, and transnational victories of the anti-corporate globalization movement have slowed the expansion of the transnational treadmill of production in numerous ways (especially in restricting access to and preventing the privatization of high-profile natural resource pools). But the movement's greatest contribution may actually be in generating an alternative, or set of possible alternatives, to the treadmill development path. Through the WSF and smaller regional fora, the movement brings together the concerns, experiences, goals, and strategies of antitreadmill activists. They seek to formulate alternative development strategies and generate political strategies for their realization.

These fora can be conceptualized as the alternative think tanks of those seeking a more socially just and ecologically sustainable future. They are by no means as well funded or organized as the think tanks that generate neoliberal ideology and policy. Yet they do powerfully and concretely deny the notion that there is only one viable development path, the path of the treadmill of production. The WSF theme "Another World Is Possible" is manifest not just in a critique of the current development regime. It is also manifest in a wealth of theoretical and practical knowledge of how to achieve more socially just and equitable development. Although the movement is not yet capable of *replacing* the treadmill of production, its work has clearly broken the unbridled march toward treadmill hegemony.

The treadmill has not been replaced transnationally or nationally (with the possible exception of Cuba). But it has been replaced locally in communities that have initiated and protected alternative development models. Local and regional autonomist development strategies, which have proliferated globally, serve as important proving grounds for nontreadmill development models and as powerful rejections of globalization. Alternative local development models have been put in place from Kerala, India, to Porto Alegre, Brazil. They experiment with radical democracy, syndicalist production, indigenous agrarian techniques, communal resource ownership, and barter economies.

In the recent past, an insurgent global treadmill with which local production could not compete had crushed such development alternatives (Schnaiberg and Gould 2000). The more recent failures of the treadmill, however, have created cultural and socioeconomic spaces for new, innovative development models to gain traction. Perhaps nowhere is this more apparent than in Argentina, where the collapse of the IMF's poster-child economy forced communities to find a means of economic survival outside the transnational treadmill. The great Argentine experimentation with autonomous development has given concrete reality to century-old anarchist theories. These innovations suggest what might be possible if people had the opportunity to devise their own economic development plans (Lewis and Klein 2005). All of the autonomist and alternative development models from Chiapas to the Andes to the Southern Cone are highly vulnerable. They must still negotiate their survival within the broader global political economy. Yet their current viability and strong base of social support indicates that socially just and ecologically sound alternatives to the treadmill are not simply theoretical musings, but are in fact concrete, achievable, and eminently doable. *Defeating* the treadmill may be much more difficult than establishing its *alternatives,* but that alternatives are readily available substantially lowers the social costs and risks associated with its dismantling. It also provides activists and ordinary denizens of the planet with the psychological satisfaction of knowing that the neoliberal model is no longer the "only game in town."

A key component of the anti–corporate globalization coalition is the participation of organized labor. In the United States, labor finally began to respond to the corporate-led assault on unions in 1995 with the election of the New Voice slate to the leadership of the AFL-CIO. The new leadership has attempted to reinvigorate organized labor as a social movement. It has also reached out to other progressive social movements domestically and transnationally (Clawson 2003). The results of this new labor militancy can be seen in the creation of the Union Summer's union-student organizing campaign, the emergence of the antisweatshop movement, the support of groups such as Jobs with Justice, and the push to include immigrant workers within the ranks of organized labor. As labor traditionally has been the primary countervailing force constraining the depredations of private capital (Derber 1998), the reinvigoration of organized labor is essential to any successful effort to mount an opposition to the treadmill.

Following the failed mobilization against NAFTA in 1994, organized labor found common cause with environmental and human rights groups in opposing neoliberal trade regimes, most notably the WTO and the FTAA (Buttel and Gould 2004). The extent to which "turtles and teamsters" can work out a common agenda for equitable and sustainable development remains to be seen. However, bridge-building organizations and projects that have emerged threaten to remove the wedge driven between environmentalists and organized workers by corporate deregulation campaigns (Gould et al. 2004). Efforts to build blue-green coalitions predate the U.S. anti-corporate globalization movement. An example of such efforts is the 1990 Redwood Summer organizing campaign lead by former labor organizer and Earth First! activist Judi Bari. In identifying a common enemy in corporate decision making that resulted in both timber industry job loss and old-growth forest liquidation, Bari's Redwood Summer mobilization foreshadowed the basis for blue-green coalitions to oppose the WTO and other treadmill-accelerating institutions (Bari 1994).

More recently, organizations and campaigns such as Just Transition, the Climate Justice campaign, the Apollo Alliance, and the International Campaign for Responsible Technology have served to facilitate dialogue and generate common agendas between environmentalists and labor (Lewis et al. 2004). Both organized labor, primarily at the national level, and the environmental global social movement, primarily at the international level, have been the key countervailing forces, respectively, constraining the negative distributional and ecological impacts of the treadmill. Bringing these two groups together through the coalition of the anti-corporate globalization movement has great potential to slow and modify the treadmill of production.

Greater attention to international labor organizing, as well as the need to counter capital at the level at which it operates, is an outgrowth of labor's participation in the anti-corporate globalization movement. NAFTA spurred U.S.-based unions to reach out to Mexican labor to fight the combined threats of job loss, wage decline, and the erosion of worker protections. Although U.S.-based unions may be among the most conservative elements in the anti-corporate globalization movement (along with mainstream environmental organizations), their participation in WSF discussions may serve to further radicalize their sense of what unions can and should do. And they have certainly facilitated greater coalition building with more radical unions throughout the world. One of the strongest critiques of the neoliberal agenda in WSF discussions was presented by the Congress of South African Trade Unions (COSATU) and the International Confederation of Free Trade Unions (ICFTU).

The broad critique of the current development trajectory emanating from international labor is significant in its opposition to the treadmill. In addition, from the WSF comes a clear recognition (at least in public statements) that both organized labor and environmentalists need each other's support to achieve the structural changes necessary to pursue their agenda(s) collectively or individually (Lewis et al. 2004). Nearly all groups at the WSF (including environmentalists) state clearly that the antineoliberal project is unachievable without the support of a revitalized transnational labor movement. The sheer size, basic interests, and potential power of organized labor make it perhaps the best vehicle for recruiting global mass support and for putting tangible pressure on capital. More interesting are the statements from labor groups themselves, recognizing that the success of their opposition to neoliberalism hinges on their ability to form coalitions with other sources of opposition (Fisher and Ponniah 2003).

The ICFTU, the World Confederation of Labour (WCL), and the European Trade Union Confederation (ETUC) have been strong supporters of, and vocal participants in, the WSF, as have the leaders of national unions from dozens of northern and southern countries. Unfortunately, although the participation of international organized labor is central to the WSF, the participation of U.S.-organized labor is not. The United Electrical, Radio and Machine Workers of America (UE), the United Steel Workers of America (USWA), the Communications Workers of America (CWA), and the International Longshore and Warehouse Union (ILWU) have all sent national leaders and rank-and-file participants to WSFs. But these unions are the rare exceptions among U.S. national labor organizations (Fisher and Ponniah 2003). Formal U.S. union participation was nearly invisible at the 2005 WSF in Porto Alegre, Brazil.

Most other U.S. union participation in the WSF occurs at the level of union *locals* and *individual* rank-and-file membership.

Much of that local union participation, including representatives from the Service Employees International Union (SEIU), Civil Service Employees Association (CSEA), and ILWU, has been organized through coalition groups such as Jobs with Justice. It is not surprising that the U.S. unions with perhaps the greatest international orientation (ILWU, CWA) and those with the greatest concern for removal of tariffs under "free-trade" regimes (USWA) would view participation in the WSF as important at the highest levels of union leadership and organization (Lewis et al. 2004). That the locals of other U.S. unions are ahead of their national organizations on the need for global action and solidarity provides some hope that such analytical insight may percolate up the union hierarchies over time. That much of the success of the U.S. labor-environmentalist coalition has been achieved at the local level (Lewis et al. 2004) indicates that the radical democratization of the U.S. labor movement would likely facilitate greater synthesis toward a sustainable development agenda.

A number of factors have eroded the legitimacy of the key supranational treadmill institutions such as the IMF, World Bank, and WTO. The Asian financial crisis and the IMF response powerfully undermined the efficacy of financial deregulation (Stiglitz 2003). The collapse of the IMF's poster child for structural adjustment policies, Argentina, has greatly increased the willingness of southern governments to question, oppose, and reject the entire policy package of acceleration of natural resource exports, privatization, and withdrawal of social welfare benefits. Successful national anti–corporate globalization campaigns such as Bolivia's "water wars" and "gas wars" have emboldened southern populations by demonstrating that the interests of transnational treadmill firms and their state supporters can be defeated when confronted directly and aggressively. The combined actions of high-profile street protests, the formation of southern state coalitions, and the schism among northern states stalled the millennial round of WTO negotiations and substantially slowed the pace of supranational treadmill institutionalization (Buttel and Gould 2004). The electoral success of FTAA opponents in Latin America and the hemispheric protests against FTAA approval have resulted in a remarkable retreat from the strong agreement supported by the United States.

Conclusion

The combined effect of these recent events has placed the direction of global development and the institutions promoting the transnational treadmill under greater scrutiny and on public agendas worldwide and at all levels. What was commonly viewed as the inevitable triumph of the treadmill in the mid-1990s is now increasingly viewed as a flawed and failed vision. This may prove no more than a temporary bump on the road to treadmill hegemony. But it may also signal that the distributional and ecological costs of the global treadmill will not be accepted, requiring the substantial alteration or replacement of the treadmill of production with a new—or, more likely, multiple new—development paths. At least in the early twenty-first century, the supranational treadmill institutions are increasingly visible and are debated and opposed in ways that were unforeseen by those who sought to use them to achieve the triumph of exchange values over use values on a global scale.

At the core of many of these antitreadmill developments is a call for meaningful radical democracy from the grass roots worldwide. This call includes shifts in the democratization of unions and natural resource decision making. It also incorporates the democratization of production through the democratization of development priorities. More widely, it entails the challenge to the international financial institutions to embrace greater democratization of national policy making. A unifying theme in global opposition to the treadmill is the empowerment of the grass roots. Most heartening is that the call for grassroots democracy is organized transnationally, which permits direct engagement with the forces organized at the transnational level, where any genuine democracy has been undermined.

Such global unity in support of local autonomy serves to counter the failures of global social movements to meaningfully connect to local constituencies, and the failures of local movements to be able to effectively access and oppose global institutions (Schnaiberg and Gould 2000).

The formal democratization of much of the world after the end of the cold war had laid bare the limits of elite-dominated democratic systems. At the same time, it increased expectations for meaningful public input into social, economic, and environmental policy. In the north, the failure of formal liberal democratic structures to respond effectively to the concerns of citizenries has similarly called the efficacy of existing "democratic" structures into question. The rallying cry for treadmill opposition may ultimately prove to be "democracy now." This would by necessity include democratic control not only of formal policy decision making but also of:

- development priorities,
- socioeconomic and environmental trade-offs,
- the distribution of costs and benefits of various development options, and
- the democratization of science and technology research priorities and trajectories.

If there is to be another world that achieves a new and sustainable synthesis between social benefits and ecological costs, direct participation by the world's population will be necessary for its creation, implementation, and acceptance. The treadmill of production retains its powerful momentum. But we can take heart in the clear indications that others have joined the battle against it. The efforts to modify or replace the treadmill may very well fail. The forces aligned in support of the treadmill—economic, military, and ideological—are incredibly powerful, well financed, and well organized. But the system is showing signs of strain, and its opponents are gaining strength ideologically, organizationally, and materially. The future of the treadmill of production therefore remains contested and triumph far from inevitable. It is our fondest hope that our intellectual work contributes in some small way to the emergence of a new environment-society synthesis and the generation of the means to realize it.

Acronyms

AFL-CIO	American Federation of Labor and Congress of Industrial Organizations
ANWR	Arctic National Wildlife Refuge
CDC	Centers for Disease Control and Prevention
CEI	Competitive Enterprise Institute
CERCLA	Comprehensive Environmental Response, Compensation, and Liability Act
CFCs	chlorofluorocarbons
COSATU	Congress of South African Trade Unions
CSEA	Civil Service Employees Association
CWA	Communication Workers of America
DoD	Department of Defense
EPA	U.S. Environmental Protection Agency
ETUC	European Trade Union Confederation
EU	European Union
FIFRA	Federal Insecticide, Fungicide, and Rodenticide Act
FTAA	Free Trade Area of the Americas
GATT	General Agreement on Tariffs and Trade
GDP	gross domestic product
GNP	gross national product
ICFTU	International Confederation of Free Trade Unions
ILWU	International Longshore and Warehouse Union
IMF	International Monetary Fund
LULU	Locally unwanted land use
NAFTA	North American Free Trade Agreement
NEPA	National Environmental Policy Act

NGO	Nongovernmental organization
OECD	Organization for Economic Cooperation and Development
PBDE	Polybrominated diphenyl ethers
RCRA	Resource Conservation and Recovery Act
SEIU	Service Employees International Union
TNC	Transnational corporation
TSMO	Transnational social movement organization
UAW	United Automobile Workers
UE	United Electrical, Radio and Machine Workers of America
USWA	United Steel Workers of America
WCL	World Conderation of Labour
WSF	World Social Forum
WTO	World Trade Organization

Notes

Note to Chapter 1

1. An earlier version of this monograph was prepared for the Symposium on Environment and the Treadmill of Production, University of Wisconsin, Madison, October 31–November 1, 2003. The comments of our colleague Adam Weinberg are gratefully acknowledged. An abbreviated version of parts of this monograph was published in *Organization and Environment* in 2004.

Notes to Chapter 2

1. Marketability refers to the producer's ability to generate a sense of need or desire for the product through advertising. We believe that markets are socially constructed and do not exist prior to marketing.
2. As environmentalists and treadmill scholars now know, a combination of production and consumption of automobiles and trucks has maintained high levels of air pollution in our urban areas. Specifically, while motor vehicles built today emit fewer pollutants (60–80 percent less, depending on the pollutant) than those built in the 1960s, cars and trucks still account for almost half the emissions of the ozone precursors—volatile organic compounds (VOCs) and nitrogen oxide (NOx)—and up to 90 percent of the carbon monoxide (CO) emissions in urban areas.
3. The Clean Air Act of 1990 establishes tighter pollution standards for emissions from automobiles and trucks. But, as with the original legislation, none of the standards will address the problem of production

and consumption, so the fundamental problem remains. Despite the significant role of consumption in this scenario, the treadmill model would likely focus on the broader political economic arrangements among the state, industry, developers, and labor in their collaboration to produce (sub)urban sprawl and metropolitan regions geared toward auto addiction and away from public transportation (Bullard et al. 2000). Thus, it would make less sense to blame the consumers for this problem when other stakeholders are in fact much more responsible.

Notes to Chapter 4

1. Special attention was given to the impacts of treadmill penetration on more socially and ecologically sustainable development paths and initiatives throughout the global south, and the mechanisms by which the treadmill would force out alternative development strategies at local and regional levels were described.

2. The call for transnational, extralocal political challenges directed at treadmill elites appeared just before the embryonic northern wing of the anti-corporate globalization movement would gain substantial social visibility, most notably three years later in November 1999 in Seattle (Buttel and Gould 2004).

Notes to Chapter 5

1. The political climate for adoption and diffusion of the treadmill model became quite hostile and difficult. Treadmill theory implies that deep structural changes in the direction of progressive distribution and growth deceleration are central to any viable solution to environmental problems. But the structural changes that were being implemented by transnational corporations, states, and international financial institutions were in a direction diametrically opposed. This made the possibility of implementing treadmill prescriptions appear less viable than ever.

2. Each of those theoretical and intellectual tacks were less threatening to careers and promised better intellectual markets. Structural analysis and neo-Marxism became decreasingly fashionable, in response to the external political realities. This was increasingly manifest in internal professional organizational pressures. In short, treadmill theory became politically and professionally inexpedient.

3. The treadmill is a theoretical framework with explanatory power, but it offers a scholarly future filled with much political conflict. Its only

long-term prospects for seriously addressing contemporary socioenvironmental crises entail sustained conflict, and this is bound to limit the
treadmill's attraction to scholars.

4. This younger generation has been exposed to difficult times following Reaganism. It has seen few viable alternative models operating in
opposition. This generation has not seen the creation of broad environmental regulatory policies and agencies. Instead, it has witnessed their
dismantlement. This generation may be more prepared intellectually
and emotionally, however, to engage in the political conflicts and intellectual challenges of the treadmill's socioenvironmental dynamic.

5. Although later iterations of treadmill theory more clearly integrated racial inequality in the model, those theoretical presentations
emerged after the environmental justice movement had already developed a strong identity and its own body of academic literature. Only
quite recently have environmental justice and treadmill theory begun
to converge (Pellow 2002), offering an important corrective to both
intellectual traditions in moving environmental justice theory toward
greater consideration of macrostructural analysis, and treadmill theory
toward greater consideration of the role played by cultural and institutional racial discrimination. Thus, one of the principal weaknesses of the
environmental justice movement has been the lack of integration in the
analysis of class and race in its framing of diagnostic (i.e., the source of
the problem) and prescriptive (i.e., possible solutions) collective action
(Pellow and Brulle 2005).

6. Nevertheless, the extent to which the movement can be said
to have overtly and consciously adopted an academic theory remains
limited. Localness of focus of much of the citizen-worker antitoxics
movement and its failure to truly develop as a conscious national and
transnational social movement restrained its analysis. Thus, the movement addressed only a limited macrostructural analytical framework,
as outlined in *Local Environmental Struggles*.

7. Southern audiences were more accustomed to seeing the necessity of structural analysis and political conflict. That cultural history,
combined with the rapid acceleration of environmental degradation in
the south, was fostered by corporate transnationalization and northern
externalization of environmental costs. A history of structural analysis
and political conflict induced environmental movements in the global
south to adopt treadmill theory overtly in their political critiques.

8. Greater access to treadmill theory through translation of theoretical works into Spanish, Portuguese, and other languages would have
facilitated the adoption of treadmill theory by the movements that
represented perhaps its best potential audience.

9. These critiques are found in a large body of academic and movement literature. The treadmill model's emphasis on the necessity of political coalition formation, overt political confrontation, and deep structural social change makes it a perfect fit with the emerging ideology, existing political strategy, and long-range goals of the anti-corporate globalization movement.

10. Hence the anti-corporate globalization movement may be creating the perfect audience for a transnationalized model of the treadmill of production. In that sense, it may be that the significant influence of treadmill theory on social movements is really just emerging.

Notes to Chapter 6

1. Studying levels of environmental concern or the public declarations by state and industry elites about their devotion to sustainability can be useful in analyzing how individuals and organizations produce discourses about and interpret environmental problems. But these approaches do not allow one to examine the root causes of the environmental crisis or even the actual outcomes of state and corporate environmental policies. If scholars want to follow this line of analysis, the treadmill is a far more useful framework.

2. This has also occurred in the case of mining and resource extractive industries (Charlier 1993).

Notes to Chapter 7

1. The three of us have evolved different political preferences and perspectives, while we all share the analytic principles of the treadmill. In a sense, this freedom is one reason scholars are attracted to beginning their studies with a framework like the treadmill.

2. While this may appear to be a new development, Chomsky (1993), however, notes that the integration of state and corporate power and interests is a phenomenon that is hundreds of years old. The corporate-state alliance is what made European imperialism possible and one of the main characteristics of contemporary imperialistic practices by the United States and other nations. While the treadmill model developed out of the post–World War II era to explain political-economic dynamics around environmental policy, it is likely that the basic social forces associated with capitalism, imperialism, and militarism would allow us to extend treadmill analyses back several centuries.

3.   During the early days of this nation's history, corporate charters were developed precisely for this purpose—to demand that private industry operate in a fashion that primarily benefits the citizenry (Mander and Goldsmith 1996). These laws are still on the books and have been invoked by human rights activists in efforts to reign in corporate abuse in a number of nations. These are efforts to redefine (or perhaps *remember*) the role of treadmill institutions in our society and to reclaim power over them.

4.   It is only by treating technological innovation as a process outside the political economy that claims for a culturally driven shift in the technological trajectory can be made. The failure to see technological innovation as an artifact and a product of a specific set of political-economic arrangements is precisely the type of analytical weakness that the treadmill seeks to correct.

5.   Daly (1996) distinguishes between *development*, which enhances the quality of social life, and economic *growth,* which improves key economic indicators such as GDP but often negatively affects the quality of social life. Economic growth then is a poor measure of enhancements to the quality of life, although the two terms are commonly used interchangeably for ideological purposes.

Note to Chapter 8

1.   The precautionary principle essentially argues that production changes must be viewed skeptically and evaluated *before* widespread adoption. In contrast, risk assessment is often carried out *after* production changes. There are both scientific and political problems with the latter approach, which has been the dominant one in the United States (Schnaiberg 1980: chs. 6–7).

References

Adeola, F. 2000. "Cross-national Environmental Justice and Human Rights Issues—A Review of Evidence in the Developing World." *American Behavioral Scientist* 43: 686–706.

Agyeman, J., R. Bullard, R. and B. Evans, eds. 2003. *Just Sustainabilities: Development in an Unequal World.* Cambridge, MA: MIT Press.

Amott, T., and J. Matthaei. 1991. *Race, Gender, and Work: A Multicultural Economic History of Women in the United States.* Boston: South End Press.

Athanasiou, T. 1996. *Divided Planet: The Ecology of Rich and Poor.* New York: Little, Brown.

Bari, J. 1994. *Timber Wars.* Monroe, ME: Common Courage Press.

Barlow, M., and T. Clarke. 2002. *Blue Gold: The Fight to Stop the Corporate Theft of the World's Water.* New York: The New Press.

Barringer, F. 2004. "Bush Record: New Priorities in Environment." *New York Times,* September 14, A1.

Beck, U. 1992. *Risk Society: Towards a New Modernity.* Translated by M. Ritter. Introduction by S. Lash and B. Wynne. Thousand Oaks, CA: Sage.

Beder, S. 1997. *Global Spin: The Corporate Assault on Environmentalism.* White River Junction, VT: Chelsea Green.

Bell, D. 1962. *The End of Ideology: On the Exhaustion of Political Ideas in the Fifties.* Cambridge, MA: Harvard University Press.

Benford, R. 2005. "The Half-Life of the Environmental Justice Frame: Innovation, Diffusion, and Stagnation." In *People, Power, and the Environment: A Critical Appraisal of the Environmental Justice Movement.* Edited by David N. Pellow and Robert J. Brulle. Cambridge, MA: MIT Press.

Blum, W. 1995. *Killing Hope: U.S. Military and CIA Interventions since World War II.* Monroe, ME: Common Courage Press.

Boggs, C. 2003. *The End of Politics: Corporate Power and the Decline of the Public Sphere.* New York: Guilford Press.

Brulle, R. 2000. *Agency, Democracy, and Nature: The U.S. Environmental Movement from a Critical Theory Perspective.* Cambridge, MA: MIT Press.

Bullard, R. D. 1990. *Dumping in Dixie: Race, Class and Environmental Quality.* Boulder, CO: Westview.

———, ed. 1993. *Confronting Environmental Racism: Voices from the Grassroots.* Boston: South End Press.

———. 2004. "25 Years Since the Start of the Environmental Justice Movement." Paper presented at the Annual Meetings of the American Sociological Association.

Bullard, R., G. S. Johnson, and A. O. Torres, eds. 2000. *Sprawl City: Race, Politics, and Planning in Atlanta.* San Francisco: Island Press.

Buncombe, A. 2004. "The Defiance of Science." *Independent* (UK), June 29.

Buttel, F. H. 1997. "Some Observations on Agro-Food Change and the Future of Agricultural Movements." In *Globalising Food: Agrarian Questions and Global Restructuring.* Edited by D. Goodman and M. Watts, 344–365. London: Routledge.

Buttel, F. H., and K. A. Gould. 2004. "Global Social Movement(s) at the Crossroads: Some Observations on the Trajectory of the Anti-corporate Globalization Movement." *Journal of World Systems Research* 10 (1): 37–66.

———. 2005. "Global Social Movements at the Crossroads: An Investigation of Relations between the Anti-corporate Globalization and Environmental Movements." In *Transforming Globalization: Challenges and Opportunities in the Post 9/11 Era.* Edited by Bruce Podobnik and Thomas Reifer. Boston, MA: Brill Academic.

Buttel, F. H., and C. Humphrey. 2002. "Sociological Theory and the Natural Environment." In *Handbook of Environmental Sociology.* Edited by R. Dunlap and W. Michelson. Westport, CT: Greenwood Press.

Carson, R. 1962. *Silent Spring.* Boston, MA: Mariner Books. 40th Anniversary Special Edition, 2002.

Centers for Disease Control (CDC). 2003, January. Second National Report on Human Exposure to Environmental Chemicals. Atlanta, GA: Centers for Disease Control and Prevention.

Charlier, M. 1993. "Going South: U.S. Mining Firms, Unwelcome at Home, Flock to Latin America." *Wall Street Journal,* June 18.

Chomsky, N. 1993. *Year 501: The Conquest Continues.* Cambridge, MA: South End Press.

Clapp, J. 2001. *Toxic Exports: The Transfer of Hazardous Wastes from Rich to Poor Countries.* Ithaca, NY: Cornell University Press.

Clarke, T. 1996. "Mechanisms of Corporate Rule." In *The Case against the Global Economy.* Edited by J. Mander and E. Goldsmith, 297–308. San Francisco: Sierra Club Books.

Clawson, D. 2003. *The Next Upsurge: Labor and the New Social Movements.* New York: Cornell University Press.

Collins, P. H. 2000. *Black Feminist Thought: Knowledge, Consciousness, and the Politics of Empowerment.* 2nd ed. London: Routledge.

Collinson, H., ed. 1996. *Green Guerrillas: Environmental Conflicts and Initiatives in Latin America and the Caribbean.* London: Monthly Review Press.

Commoner, B. 1977. *The Poverty of Power: Energy and the Economic Crisis.* New York: Bantam Books.

Crenshaw, A. B. 2003. "Review of D. Shipler [2004]. *The Working Poor: Invisible in America* (New York: Alfred Knopf)." *Washington Post,* January 23, E1.

Daly, H. 1996. *Beyond Growth: The Economics of Sustainable Development.* Boston: Beacon Press.

Danaher, K., ed. 2001. *Democratizing the Global Economy: The Battle against the World Bank and the IMF.* Monroe, ME: Common Courage Press.

Danaher, K., and R. Burbach, eds. 2000. *Globalize This: The Battle against the World Trade Organization and Corporate Rule.* Monroe, ME: Common Courage Press.

Daykin, N., and L. Doyal, eds. 1999. *Health and Work: Critical Perspectives.* New York: St. Martin's Press.

Derber, C. 1998. *Corporation Nation: How Corporations Are Taking Over Our Lives and What We Can Do about It.* New York: St. Martin's Griffin.

Domhoff, G. W. 1998. *Who Rules America? Power and Politics in the Year 2000.* Mountain View, CA: Mayfield.

Dowie, M. 1995. *Losing Ground: American Environmentalism at the Close of the Twentieth Century.* Cambridge, MA: MIT Press.

Dunlap, R. E., and A. G. Mertig, eds. 1992. *American Environmentalism: The U.S. Environmental Movement, 1970–1990.* Bristol, PA: Crane, Russak.

Dunlap, R., and W. Michelson, eds. 2002. *Handbook of Environmental Sociology.* Westport, CT: Greenwood Press.

Ehrlich, P. 1971. *The Population Bomb.* New York: Ballantine.

Environment News Service (ENS). 2003. "Toxic Substances Put One in Five EU Workers at Risk." ENS, May 16.

———. 2004a. "Bush Highlights Volunteers' Role in Environmental Protection." *Environment News Service,* April 26.

———. 2004b. "Environmental Spending on U.S. Army Bases Halted." *Environment News Service,* May 28.

————. 2004c. "EPA Sued over Secret Meetings with Chemical Companies." *Environment News Service*, January 16.

————. 2004d. "Superfund Shortfall Leaves Communities Exposed to Toxic Waste." *Environment News Service*, January 8.

Faber, D., and E. Krieg, 2001. *Unequal Exposure to Ecological Hazards: Environmental Injustices in the Commonwealth of Massachusetts.* Boston, MA: Northeastern University Press.

Fisher, W. F., and T. Ponniah. 2003. *Another World Is Possible: Popular Alternatives to Globalization at the World Social Forum.* New York: Zed.

Florini, A. M. 2000. *The Third Force: The Rise of Transnational Civil Society.* Washington, DC: Carnegie Endowment for International Peace.

Fox, J. A., and L. D. Brown. 1998. *The Struggle for Accountability: The World Bank, NGOs, and Grassroots Movements.* Cambridge: Massachusetts Institute of Technology Press.

Garcia Johnson, R. 2000. *Exporting Environmentalism: U.S. Multinational Chemical Corporations in Brazil and Mexico.* Cambridge: Massachusetts Institute of Technology Press.

Gedicks, A. 1993. *The New Resource Wars: Native and Environmental Struggles against Multinational Corporations.* Boston: South End Press.

————. 2001. *Resource Rebels: Native Challenges to Mining and Oil Corporations.* Cambridge, MA: South End Press.

George, S., G. Monbiot, L. German, T. Hayter, A. Callinicos, and K. Moody. 2001. *Anti-capitalism: A Guide to the Movement.* London: Bookmarks.

Glaser, B., and A. Strauss, 1967. *Discovery of Grounded Theory: Strategies for Qualitative Research.* New York: Aldine de Gruyter.

Goldman, B. 1991. *The Truth about Where You Live: An Atlas for Action on Toxins and Mortality.* New York: Times Books/Random House.

Goldman, M., ed. 1998. *Privatizing Nature: Political Struggles for the Global Commons.* New Brunswick, NJ: Rutgers University Press; London: Pluto Press.

————. 2005. *Imperial Nature: The World Bank and the Struggle for Social Justice in the Age of Globalization.* New Haven: Yale University Press.

Gonzalez, G. 2001. *Corporate Power and the Environment.* New York: Rowman and Littlefield.

Goodman, A. 2003. *Exception to the Rulers: Exposing Oily Politicians, War Profiteers, and the Media That Love Them.* New York: Hyperion.

Gould, K. A. 1988. "The Politicization of Science in the Environmental Impact Statement Process." *Wisconsin Sociologist* 25 (4): 139-143.

————. 1991. "The Sweet Smell of Money: Economic Dependency and Local Environmental Political Mobilization." *Society and Natural Resources* 4 (2): 133-150.

―――. 1992. "Putting the [W]R.A.P.s on Public Participation: Remedial Action Planning and Working-Class Power in the Great Lakes." *Sociological Practice Review* 3 (3): 133–139.

―――. 1993. "Pollution and Perception: Social Visibility and Local Environmental Political Mobilization." *Qualitative Sociology* 16 (2): 157–178.

―――. 1994. "Legitimacy and Growth in the Balance: The Role of the State in Environmental Remediation." *Industrial and Environmental Crisis Quarterly* 8, 237–256.

―――. 1999. "Tactical Tourism: A Comparative Analysis of Rainforest Tourism in Ecuador and Belize." *Organization and Environment* 12 (3): 245–262.

―――. 2003. "Transnational Environmentalism, Power and Development in Belize." *Belizean Studies* 25 (2): 59–70.

―――. 2006. "Promoting Sustainability." In *Public Sociologies Reader.* Edited by J. Blau and K. L. Smith, 213–229. New York: Rowman and Littlefield.

―――. 2007. "The Ecological Costs of Militarization." *Peace Review* 19 (3): 331–334.

Gould, K. A., T. Lewis, and J. T. Roberts. 2004. "Blue-green Coalitions: Constraints and Possibilities in the Post 9-11 Political Environment." *Journal of World Systems Research* 10 (1): 90–116.

Gould, K. A., T. Lewis, and J. T. Roberts. 2005. "Blue-Green Coalitions: Constraints and Possibilities in the Post 9-11 Political Environment." In *Transformaing Globalization: Challenges and Opportunites in the Post 9/11 Era.* Edited by B. Podobnik and T. Reifer. Boston: Brill Academic Press, 123–138.

Gould, K. A., Schnaiberg, A., and Weinberg, A. S. 1995. "Natural Resource Use in a Transnational Treadmill: International Agreements, National Citizenship Practices, and Sustainable Development." *Humboldt Journal of Social Relations* 2 (1): 61–93.

―――. 1996. *Local Environmental Struggles: Citizen Activism in the Treadmill of Production.* Cambridge, UK: Cambridge University Press.

GroundWork. 2002. *The GroundWork Report: Corporate Accountability in South Africa.* GroundWork: Pietermaritzburg, South Africa.

Gurr, T. 1971. *Why Men Rebel.* Princeton, NJ: Princeton University Press.

Hardt, M., and A. Negri. 2001. *Empire.* Cambridge, MA: Harvard University Press.

Harris, P. 2003. "Bush Covers Up Climate Research." *The Observer,* September 21.

Harrison, B. 1994. *Lean and Mean: The Changing Landscape of Corporate Power in the Age of Flexibility.* New York: Basic Books.

Hawken, P. 2007. *Blessed Unrest: How the Largest Movement in the World Came into Being and Why No One Saw It Coming.* New York: Viking Press.

Hays, S. 2003. *Flat Broke with Children: Women in the Age of Welfare Reform.* New York: Oxford University Press.

Hilz, C. 1992. *The International Toxic Waste Trade.* New York: Van Nostrand Reinhold.

Homer-Dixon, T. F. 2001. *Environment, Scarcity, and Violence.* Princeton, NJ: Princeton University Press.

Hooks, G., and C. L. Smith. 2004. "The Treadmill of Destruction: National Sacrifice Areas and Native Americans." *American Sociological Review* 69: 558-575.

Hurley, A. 1995. *Environmental Inequalities: Race, Class, and Industrial Pollution in Gary, Indiana, 1945-1980.* Chapel Hill: University of North Carolina Press.

Huws, U. 1999. "Material World: The Myth of the 'Weightless Economy.'" In *Socialist Register.* Edited by L. Panitch, and C. Leys. New York: Monthly Review Press.

Johnson, C. 2000. *Blowback: The Costs and Consequences of American Empire.* New York: Henry Holt.

Kagarlitsky, B. 2001. "Facing the Crisis." *Links* 19.

Kazis, R., and R. Grossman. 1982. *Fear at Work: Job Blackmail, Labor and the Environment.* New York: Pilgrim Press.

Keck, M. E., and K. Sikkink. 1998. *Activists beyond Borders: Advocacy Networks in International Politics.* Ithaca, NY: Cornell University Press.

Khagram, S., J. V. Riker, and K. Sikkink, eds. 2002. *Restructuring World Politics: Transnational Social Movements, Networks, and Norms.* Minneapolis: University of Minnesota Press.

Korten, D. 2001. *When Corporations Rule the World.* Bloomfield, CT: Kumarian Press.

Krugman, P. 2002. "For Richer." *New York Times Magazine,* October 20.

———. 2003. *The Great Unraveling: Losing Our Way in the New Century.* New York: W. W. Norton.

LaDuke, W. 1999. *All Our Relations: Native Struggles for Land and Life.* Cambridge, MA: South End Press.

Leicht, K. T., and S. T. Fitzgerald. 2007. *Postindustrial Peasants: The Illusion of Middle-Class Prosperity.* New York: Worth.

Lewis, A., and N. Klein. 2005. *The Take.* Documentary. New York: First Run Features.

Lewis, T. L. 2003. "Environmental Aid: Driven by Recipient Need or Donor Interest?" *Social Science Quarterly* 84(1): 144-161.

———. 2000. "Transnational Conservation Movement Organizations: Shaping the Protected Area Systems of Less Developed Countries." *Mobilization: An International Journal of Research and Theory about Social Movements, Protest, and Collective Behavior* 5(1):105-123.

Lewis, T., K. A. Gould, and J. T. Roberts. 2004. "From Blue-Green Coalitions to Blue-Green Partnerships? Creating Enduring Institutions through Just Transition, Climate Justice and the World Social Forum." Paper presented at the annual meeting of the American Sociological Association, San Francisco.

Lindblom, C. E. 1977. *Politics and Markets: The World's Political-Economic Systems.* New York: Basic Books.

Lowi, T. 1979. *The End of Liberalism.* 2nd ed. New York: W. W. Norton.

Lukes, S. 1974. *Power: A Radical View.* London: Macmillan.

Luoma, J. 2003. "Toxic Immunity." *Mother Jones,* November/December: 21–23.

Mander, J., and E. Goldsmith, eds. 1996. *The Case against the Global Economy.* San Francisco: Sierra Club Books.

McDonald, D., ed. 2002. *Environmental Justice in South Africa.* Athens, OH: Ohio University Press.

McMichael, P. 2004. *Development and Social Change: A Global Perspective,* 3rd ed. Thousand Oaks, CA: Pine Forge Press.

McNeil, B. 1998. "City Tries to Trash Illegal Dumping in Austin." *Austin Weekly News,* June 4.

Melosi, M. 2001. *Effluent America: Cities, Industry, Energy and the Environment.* Pittsburgh: University of Pittsburgh Press.

Mertes, T., ed. 2004. *A Movement of Movements: Is Another World Really Possible?* New York: Verso.

Mills, C. W. 1959. *The Sociological Imagination.* New York: Oxford.

Mitchell, R. C. 1980. "How 'Soft,' 'Deep,' or 'Left'? Present Constituencies in the Environmental Movement." *Natural Resources Journal* 20 (April): 345–358.

Mol, A. P. J. 1995. *The Refinement of Production: Ecological Modernization Theory and the Dutch Chemical Industry.* Ultrecht: Jan van Arkel/International Books.

Mol, A. P. J., and G. Spaargaren. 2000. "Ecological Modernization Theory in Debate: A Review." In *Ecological Modernization around the World.* Edited by A. P. J. Mol and D. A. Sonnenfeld, 17–49. London: Frank Cass.

Morrison, D. E. 1986. "How and Why Environmental Consciousness Has Trickled Down." In *Distributional Conflicts in Environmental-Resource Policy.* Edited by A. Schnaiberg, N. Watts, and K. Zimmermann, 187–220. New York: St. Martin's/Aldershot, UK: Gower.

Moyers, B. 1990. *Global Dumping Ground: The International Traffic in Hazardous Waste.* Washington, DC: Seven Locks Press.

Mumford, L. 1963. *Technics and Civilization.* New York: Harcourt Brace Jovanovich.

Noble, D. F. 1977. *America by Design: Science, Technology, and the Rise of Corporate Capitalism.* New York: Alfred A. Knopf.

Obach, B. 2004. *Labor and the Environmental Movement: The Quest for Common Ground.* Cambridge, MA: MIT Press.

Oliver, M., and T. Shapiro. 1995. *Black Wealth, White Wealth: A New Perspective on Racial Inequality.* New York: Routledge.

Palmer, P. 2005. "The Pen Is Mightier Than the Sword: Global Environmental Justice One Letter at a Time." Interview with D. N. Pellow. In *Power, Justice, and the Environment: A Critical Appraisal of the Environmental Justice Movement.* Edited by D. N. Pellow and R. J. Brulle. Cambridge: Massachusetts Institute of Technology Press.

Park, L. S. 2003. "Citizenship through Consumption: Children of Asian Immigrant Entrepreneurs." Paper presented at the Association of Asian American Studies, San Francisco, May.

Pegg, J. R. 2004. "Justice Scalia Dismisses Sierra Club Recusal Request." *Environment News Service,* March 19, http://www.ens-newswire.com/ens/mar2004/2004-03-19-10.asp. Accessed March 20, 2004.

Pellow, D. N. 1999. "Framing Emerging Environmental Movement Tactics: Mobilizing Consensus, De-mobilizing Conflict." *Sociological Forum* 14: 659–683.

———. 2001. "Environmental Justice and the Political Process: Movements, Corporations, and the State. *The Sociological Quarterly* 42: 47–67.

———. 2002. *Garbage Wars: The Struggle for Environmental Justice in Chicago.* Cambridge: Massachusetts Institute of Technology Press.

Pellow, D. N., and R. J. Brulle, eds. 2005. *Power, Justice, and the Environment: A Critical Appraisal of the Environmental Justice Movement.* Cambridge: Massachusetts Institute of Technology Press.

Pellow, D. N., and L. S. Park. 2002. *The Silicon Valley of Dreams: Environmental Injustice, Immigrant Workers, and the High-Tech Global Economy.* New York: New York University Press.

Phillips, B. 2008. *Armageddon or Evolution? The Scientific Method and Escalating World Problems.* Boulder, CO: Paradigm Publishers.

Phillips, B., and L. C. Johnston. 2007. *The Invisible Crisis of Modern Society: Reconstructing Sociology's Paradigmatic Assumptions.* Boulder, CO: Paradigm Publishers.

Philo, G., and D. Miller, eds. 2001. *Market Killing: What the Free Market Does and What Social Scientists Can Do about It.* New York: Longman.

Piven, F. F., and R. Cloward. 1979. *Poor People's Movements: Why They Succeed, How They Fail.* New York: Vintage.

Price, D. D. 1986. *Little Science, Big Science—and Beyond.* New York: Columbia University Press.

Pulido, L. 2000. "Rethinking Environmental Racism." *Annals of the Association of American Geographers* 90: 12–40.

Redclift, M. 1987. *Sustainable Development: Exploring the Contradictions.* New York: Routledge.

Reich, R. 1991. *The Work of Nations: Preparing Ourselves for 21st Century Capitalism.* New York: Alfred A. Knopf.

Roberts, T., and M. Toffolon-Weiss. 2000. *Chronicles from the Environmental Justice Frontline.* Cambridge, UK: Cambridge University Press.

Roy, A. 2004. "Tide or Ivory Snow? Public Power in the Age of Empire." Address to the American Sociological Association, San Francisco, August 16.

Rubin, B. 1995. *Shifts in the Social Contract: Understanding Change in American Society.* Thousand Oaks, CA: Pine Forge Press.

Rudel, T. K. 1993. *Tropical Deforestation: Small Farmers and Land Clearing in the Ecuadorian Amazon.* New York: Columbia University Press.

St. Clair, J. 2007. "The Withering of the American Environmental Movement: The Thrill Is Gone." *Counterpunch,* Weekend Edition, February 3/4.

Schiller, H. I. 1996. *Information Inequality: The Deepening Social Crisis in America.* New York: Routledge.

Schnaiberg, A. 1973. "Politics, Participation and Pollution: The 'Environmental Movement.'" In *Cities in Change: Studies on the Urban Condition.* Edited by J. Walton and D. E. Carns, 605–627. Boston: Allyn and Bacon.

———. 1975. "Social Syntheses of the Societal-Environmental Dialectic: The Role of Distributional Impacts." *Social Science Quarterly* (June): 5–20.

———. 1977. "Obstacles to Environmental Research by Scientists and Technologists: A Social Structural Analysis." *Social Problems* (June): 500–520.

———. 1980. *The Environment: From Surplus to Scarcity.* New York: Oxford University Press.

———. 1986. "The Role of Experts and Mediators in the Channeling of Distributional Conflict." In *Distributional Conflicts in Environmental-Resource Policy.* Edited by A. Schnaiberg, N. Watts, and K. Zimmermann, 363–379. New York: St. Martin's/Aldershot, UK: Gower.

———. 1994. "The Political Economy of Environmental Problems and Policies: Consciousness, Coordination, and Control Capacity." In *Advances in Human Ecology.* Edited by L. Freese. Vol. 3: 23–64. Greenwich, CT: JAI Press.

———. 2004. "Economy and the Environment." In *The Handbook of Economic Sociology.* Edited by N. Smelser and R. Swedberg, 703–726. Princeton, NJ: Princeton University Press.

Schnaiberg, A., and K. A. Gould. 2000. *Environment and Society: The Enduring Conflict.* West Caldwell, NJ: Blackburn Press.

Schnaiberg, A., D. N. Pellow, and A. S. Weinberg. 2002. "The Treadmill of Production and the Environmental State." In *The Environmental*

State under Pressure. A. P. J. Mol and F. H. Buttel, 15–32. Amsterdam: Elsevier Science.

Schor, J., and D. B. Holt, eds. 2000. *The Consumer Society Reader*. New York: New Press.

Schumacher, E. F. 1973. *Small Is Beautiful: Economics as If People Mattered*. New York: Harper and Row.

Shiva, V. 2002. *Water Wars: Privatization, Pollution, and Profit*. Cambridge, MA: South End Press.

Shuman, M. 1998. *Going Local: Creating Self-Reliant Communities in a Global Age*. New York: The Free Press.

Sklair, L. 2002. *The Transnational Capitalist Class*. Oxford, UK: Blackwell.

Skocpol, T. 1980. "Political Response to Capitalist Crisis: Neo-Marxist Theories of the State and the Case of the New Deal." *Politics and Society* 10 (2): 155–201.

Sonnenfeld, D. A. 2000. "Contradictions in Ecological Modernization: Pulp and Paper Manufacturing in South-east Asia." In *Ecological Modernization around the World*. Edited by A. P. J. Mol and D. A. Sonnenfeld, 235–256. London: Frank Cass.

South Commission. 1990. *The Challenge to the South*. New York: Oxford University Press.

Spaargaren, G. 1997. *The Ecological Modernization of Production and Consumption*. PhD diss., Landbouw University, The Netherlands.

Spaargaren, G., and A. P. J. Mol. 1992. "Sociology, Environment, and Modernity: Ecological Modernisation as a Theory of Social Change." *Society and Natural Resources* 5 (4): 323–344.

Stiglitz, J. E. 2003. *Globalization and Its Discontents*. New York: W. W. Norton.

Stretton, H. 1976. *Capitalism, Socialism and the Environment*. New York: Cambridge University Press.

Szasz, A. 1994. *EcoPopulism: Toxic Waste and the Movement for Environmental Justice*. Minneapolis: University of Minnesota Press.

———. 2007. *Shopping Our Way to Safety: How We Changed from Protecting the Environment to Protecting Ourselves*. Minneapolis: University of Minnesota Press.

Taylor, B., ed. 1995. *Ecological Resistance Movements: The Emergence of Radical and Popular Environmentalism*. Albany, NY: SUNY Press.

Tilly, C. 1978. *From Mobilization to Revolution*. Reading, MA: Addison-Wesley.

Tsoukalas, T., and K. A. Gould. 1997. "Environmentalism and Organizational Dissent within the State." *Humanity and Society* 21 (3): 284–306.

United Church of Christ. 1987. *Toxic Wastes and Race in the United States*. New York: United Church of Christ Commission for Racial Justice.

United Nations Conference on Trade and Development. 1998. *Least Developed Countries 1998 Report: Overview.* Geneva: United Nations Conference on Trade and Development.

Vagts, A. 1937. *A History of Militarism.* New York: W. W. Norton.

Wallach, L., and P. Woodall. 2004. *Whose Trade Organization? A Comprehensive Guide to the WTO.* New York: The New Press.

Walsh, E., R. Warland, and D. C. Smith. 1997. *Don't Burn It Here: Grassroots Challenges to Trash Incinerators.* University Park: Pennsylvania State University Press.

Walton, J., and D. Seddon. 1994. *Free Markets and Food Riots: The Politics of Global Adjustment.* Oxford, UK: Blackwell.

Wayne, L. 2001. "Ex-Alcoa Boss May Become a Man of Steel." *New York Times,* July 17.

Weinberg, A. S. 1997. "Power and Public Policy: Community Right-to-Know and the Empowerment of People, Places, and Producers." *Humanity and Society* 21(3): 241–256.

Weinberg, A. S., D. N. Pellow, and A. Schnaiberg. 1996. "Sustainable Development as a Sociologically Defensible Concept: From Foxes and Rovers to Citizen-Workers." In *Advances in Human Ecology.* Edited by L. Freese. Vol. 5: 261–302. Westport, CT: JAI Press.

Weinberg, A. S, and A. Schnaiberg. 2001. "Globalization and Energy Policy: The Critical Role of the State and Its Constituencies." Paper presented to Kyoto Conference on Environmental Sociology, Kyoto, Japan, October.

Weinberg, A. S., D. N. Pellow, and A. Schnaiberg. 2000. *Urban Recycling and the Search for Sustainable Community Development.* Princeton, NJ: Princeton University Press.

Westra, L., and B. E. Lawson, eds. 2001. *Faces of Environmental Racism: Confronting Issues of Global Justice.* 2nd ed. Lanham, MD: Rowman and Littlefield.

White, G., ed. 2000. *Campus Inc.* Albany, NY: Prometheus.

York, R., and E. Rosa. 2003. "Key Challenges to Ecological Modernization Theory: Institutional Efficacy, Case Study Evidence, Units of Analysis, and the Pace of Eco-Efficiency." *Organization and Environment* 16: 273–288.

Index

Aadland, Anders, 97
activism, 60, 73-74, 79-80
AFL-CIO, 110
Alinsky, Saul, 59
American Sociological
    Association, 56
Anti-Privatization
    Forum, 104
antitreadmill trends,
    101-104, 114-115
ANWR. *See* Arctic Na-
    tional Wildlife Refuge
Apollo Alliance, 111
Arctic National Wildlife
    Refuge (ANWR), 92-93

Bari, Judi, 111
Basel Convention, 102
boycotts, 22
Bretton Woods institu-
    tions, 107-108
Bullard, Robert, 67
Busch, Lawrence, 96
Bush, George W., 92; re-
    election of, 98-99; sup-
    ply-side economics and,
    91; tax cuts of, 33, 90
Buttel, Frederick, 47

campaign contribu-
    tions, 50
capital investment, 10, 11
capitalism, 73, 81-82
capital mobilization, 19
capital productivity,
    decline of, 14

CEI. *See* Competitive
    Enterprise Institution
Centers for Disease
    Control and Preven-
    tion (CDC), 36-37
Cheney, Dick, 92-93
citizen-workers, 23; anti-
    toxics movement and,
    59; recycling and, 25;
    redistribution and, 85
civil rights move-
    ments, 58-59
Civil Service Employees
    Association (CSEA), 113
Clarke, Tony, 35
class, 13-15; divisions,
    33-35; environmental
    movements and, 58-50;
    inequality, 70-72; mid-
    dle, 13, 78-79; politics
    and, 90; race *v.*, 67-75
Clean Air Act, 26, 97-98
Clinton, Bill, 78, 89-90
collective action, 23
collective bargaining, 26
commodity chains, 24
Commoner, Barry, 14
Communications Workers
    of America (CWA), 112
community "right-to-
    know" policies, 78
competition, 81-82, 90-91
Competitive Enterprise
    Institution (CEI), 93-94
Comprehensive Envi-
    ronmental Response,

Compensation, and
    Liability Act, 97-98
computers, recy-
    cling of, 24-25
Congressional Bud-
    get Office, 33
Congress of South
    African Trade Unions
    (COSATU), 112
consciousness: Barry
    Commoner and, 14;
    construction and de-
    struction of, 6-7; rais-
    ing, 87; studying, 5-6
consumer debt, 32
consumers: behavior,
    21; choices, 20-22,
    23-24, 26, 83. *See*
    also citizen-workers
consumption: mass, 21;
    personal, 27; pressure,
    22-23; production *v.*,
    20, 26-27; reducing,
    81
convergence, 105
cooperative agree-
    ments, 81-82
corporate-state alliances,
    73-74, 79, 94-97
cosmetology, 5
crises, 104-113

debt, 41-42, 53
deceleration, 24
decision making, 22-23
deficits, 91

137

About the Authors

Kenneth A. Gould is Professor and Chair of the Department of Sociology at Brooklyn College and Professor of Sociology at the CUNY Graduate Center. His books include *Local Environmental Struggles: Citizen Activism in The Treadmill of Production,* with Allan Schnaiberg and Adam S. Weinberg.

David N. Pellow, Professor of Ethnic Studies at the University of California, San Diego, is the author of several books, including *Resisting Global Toxics: Transnational Movements for Environmental Justice.*

Allan Schnaiberg, Professor Emeritus of Sociology at Northwestern University, is the influential author of many books and scholarly articles.